THROUGH THE PAGES

CW00485014

With my older sister Betty in 1929

THROUGH THE PAGES
OF MY LIFE

And my Encounters
with Beatrix Potter

WILLOW TAYLOR

Alas that Spring should vanish with the Rose!
That Youth's sweet-scented Manuscript should close!
The Nightingale that in the Branches sang,
Ah, whence, and whither flown again, who knows!
(from *The Rubaiyat of Omar Khayyam*)

*To Lauren
with Best Wishes
from
Willow Taylor.*

The Beatrix Potter Society
London

Dedicated to my three children
Helen, John and Jane

First published in 2000 by The Beatrix Potter Society
Reprinted 2005
Text copyright © 2000 Willow Taylor
and The Beatrix Potter Society

Edited by Judy Taylor

Original copyright in Beatrix Potter's illustrations
© Frederick Warne & Co., 1908, 1909, 1918, 1987

Cover photograph:
Willow Taylor with Susie in Near Sawrey in 1991
Photograph copyright © Ian O'Leary 1991

Our grateful thanks for permission to use the following extracts in
the text: *Beatrix Potter's Letters – A Selection by Judy Taylor*
Copyright © Frederick Warne & Co., 1989; *The Journal of Beatrix Potter,
1881–1897* Copyright © Frederick Warne & Co., 1966, 1989;
Cousin Beatie by Ulla Hyde Parker Copyright © Ulla Hyde Parker 1981;
'Young Mind' from *You have a minute, Lord?* by David Kossoff
Copyright © David Kossoff 1977, published by Robson Books

Illustration Acknowledgements:
Beatrix Potter Society, 6; Ann Beckett, 84; Pat Bell, 81; Ethel Byers, 13, 22;
Betty Cockman, 12; Sarah Cutforth, 55; F. Warne & Co., 8 (below),
17, 18, 25, 33, 61, 75, 80, 87; Frederick Warne Archive, 23;
Mollie Green, 28; Betty Hodgson, 38, 52; Jacqueline Mock, 69;
National Trust, 17; Joan Newby, 29; Private Collector, 53;
Barry Simmons, 35, 40; Devoke Spence, 32; Amanda Thistlethwaite, 76.
All other photographs are the property of Willow Taylor.

ISBN 1 869980 17 4

Printed in Great Britain by
CPI Bath

CONTENTS

Beatrix Potter as a young girl

FOREWORD

I have had many requests to write a book about my childhood in Sawrey when Beatrix Potter was alive, so I finally decided to write down the memories and anecdotes of my early days, up to Beatrix Potter's death in 1943 when I was twenty years old. Then I was asked to bring the story forward. It does not pretend to be a great masterpiece of literary work, but I do aim to give some pleasure and information to my readers, and hope they will derive a true picture of the real Beatrix Potter from these pages.

In her *Journal* entry for 17 November 1896 Beatrix Potter wrote, 'I remember I used to half believe and wholly play with fairies when I was a child. What heaven can be more real than to retain the spirit-world of childhood, tempered and balanced by knowledge and common-sense, to fear no longer the terror that flieth by night, yet to feel truly and understand a little, a very little, of the story of life.'

I love this passage, and I think it is sad that Beatrix Potter had such a solitary childhood; but on the other hand we might have been denied her wonderful children's stories if she had been allowed a normal childhood with friends and playing children's games.

WILLOW TAYLOR

I would like to express my most sincere thanks to Judy Taylor for all her untiring help and encouragement in this project; and also to Libby Joy, who assisted her.

Tower Bank Arms as it was in 1937

Tower Bank Arms as drawn by
Beatrix Potter for *The Tale of
Jemima Puddle-Duck* in 1905

1.

THE JOURNEY BEGINS

I was born in Staveley, near Kendal, on 13 May 1923, to Margaret Browne Rawes and William Edward Burns. I was their second daughter, my sister Betty, born on 23 June 1921, being two years older. A freak snowstorm was raging at the time of my birth and the doctor, who had to drive from Kendal, was delayed by having to stop to put chains on his car. I was brought to live in Near Sawrey very soon after I was born, and to me it is the dearest place on earth. As Beatrix Potter wrote in her *Journal* in 1896, 'It is as nearly perfect a little place as I ever lived in, and such nice old-fashioned people in the village.'

I have so many happy memories of both Near Sawrey and Far Sawrey, so called because of their respective distances from Hawkshead, which was an important wool-marketing town in the eleventh and twelfth centuries. Near Sawrey is two miles beyond Hawkshead on the way to the ferry across Windermere, and Far Sawrey is half a mile further along the road. Near Sawrey was, and still is, a most beautiful Lakeland village, nestling midst the hills between two lakes, Windermere and Esthwaite Water. It was the perfect environment in which to enjoy a happy childhood.

I was brought up in the Tower Bank Arms, the inn situated on the southern edge of the village and next door to Hill Top Farm, which Beatrix Potter had bought in 1905. My parents were the tenants of the inn for thirty-five years, and the building looks almost exactly the same today as it did in Beatrix Potter's illustration for *The Tale of Jemima Puddle-Duck,* a large, rambling old house with lots of nooks and crannies.

The kitchen was then the hub of the household, with the whole of life, business and leisure, conducted from there. It was a large room with a floor of blue flagstones on which, after it had been newly scrubbed, we were not allowed to walk until it was dry, which always seemed somewhat of a bother to my sister and me. At one end of the room was a huge, black, Herald range on which all the cooking was done and all the water heated. The range was also an open fire to heat the room. Above it was a very wide mantelpiece loaded with brass and copper-ware, flanked on one side by a grandfather clock and on the other by a corner cupboard. When we played hide-and-seek I loved to get inside the grandfather clock, but unfortunately I always stopped the clock, so I was very easily found. Another favourite hiding-place was behind the pantry door, especially on baking days, when the shelves were crowded with apple pies, custard pies, bread rolls and tea-cakes straight from the oven. Again, the seekers always knew where to find me.

There was also a magnificent old walnut piano in the kitchen. My mother loved music and, when she was young, she and her sisters had been members of the Ambleside Operatic Society. She was always singing songs from the Gilbert and Sullivan operas, especially *The Mikado,* and although she could not read music, she played by ear and loved a good old sing-song round the piano. I had music lessons from Lilian Kellet who lived in a cottage between Near Sawrey and Hawkshead, a walk of a mile there and back, but I practised at home on our own piano. For me, a child who loved to romp, climb trees, and play ball games, it was sheer torture to have to go through those scales time after time, making no tune at all but hearing my friends' voices as they played outside. What a relief it was when a visitor arrived in the middle of a lesson and my mother said, 'You may go out and play for an hour, but then it will be time for bed.' That hour always passed far too quickly.

Our playground in those days was the main road through the village which ran past the inn. On many occasions, when we were playing cricket, rounders or tennis our ball would be knocked over the wall into Post Office Meadow, the field opposite Hill Top and owned by Beatrix Potter. Invariably I would be the one climbing the wall to retrieve the ball just as she was coming along from Castle Cottage, where she lived with her husband William Heelis, to visit Hill Top. Then I was in trouble.

'Why can't you use the gate? Why must you climb the wall?', she would say in her rather high-pitched voice. 'You are a naughty little girl.'

But the gate was fifty yards away and it was much quicker, and easier, and more enjoyable to climb the wall. Of course, I would never have dared to answer back but I did mutter away a bit to myself under my breath. Then Beatrix Potter (or Mrs Heelis, as we all knew her) would go to my father and tell him how naughty I was. I would usually be called inside at once, and that ended my fun for the day. Although my father was very strict with us, he was a kind and thoughtful man and did not appreciate idle gossip. As well as being the landlord, he drove the village taxi when he was not 'on duty'. He also had a pony called Peggy, which I tried to ride but she threw me off – when she was startled by a car. Peggy bolted over a gate and went straight into Esthwaite Water! No damage was done.

Near Sawrey was truly an idyllic village in the 1920s and 30s, a children's paradise. We had the freedom of the woods, the fields, the rivers and the footpaths. We were close to nature and were able to study the birds, the trees and the wild flowers as each one heralded in a new season. One year, at the village school in Far Sawrey, we entered a national bird and tree

My parents in 1928

Sawrey School as I remember it in 1933

competition. Each pupil chose a tree and a bird to study throughout the year, recording their growth and habits. It was one of my very favourite projects. I chose the song thrush and the oak tree. The song thrush is a garden bird and has a superb song. Nesting in the hedgerows it lays four to five eggs, each one blue and spotted with black. A year-round resident in this country, its presence is discovered when you find a 'thrush's anvil', a collection of broken snail shells next to a stone on the garden path. The oak tree is the monarch of the forest, from whose humble acorns came the timber for Nelson's navy. The oak leaf is also the symbol for the National Trust, chosen because as a huge oak tree grows from a very small acorn, so from very small beginnings (three people) an international organisation has grown.

Sawrey school had only two classrooms, with one teacher for the four-to-seven-year-olds and one teacher for the eight-to-fourteen-year-olds. The numbers in each class varied from year to year but there were usually about twelve children in the infants' class and about thirty in the juniors. Miss

Glover, who taught the infants, was such a dear, kind lady, just the sort of person you never forget. She was so gentle, with endless patience and understanding. I am sure it was her basic teaching which gave me the solid foundation on which to build my future education. I remember so well when I told her I was going to the pictures (to see a film) in Bowness. She said, 'I see new pictures every day when I am walking to school. If you look around you, you will see them, too. They are the most beautiful pictures.' How right she was. Above everything else she taught us observation. I never wanted to move up into Miss Jones's classroom. She was the headmistress and she had quite a different personality.

There was, of course, no television when I was young. We made our own entertainment, and the village school was regularly converted into a little theatre. All the desks were pushed to one end of the larger classroom and covered with boards to form the stage. Brown velvet curtains were hung across the front of the stage, with a backdrop of grey curtains. The smaller room was used for dressing and make-up, and the refreshments were prepared in the cloakroom. Admission prices were two shillings for the front rows, one shilling for the middle rows, and sixpence for the back rows. On the night of the performances the hall was always full, and I must

This group of local men was one of our favourite entertainments

13

say the audiences were very responsive and certainly got their money's worth.

The Dandy Coons show was the great favourite. Major Rothwell, a millionaire who lived in a large mansion called Broom Riggs between Near Sawrey and Hawkshead, led this group of minstrels who gave performances in the villages over a wide area. The members of the group were all local men, and Lilian Kellet, my music teacher, was their accompanist on the piano. At the end of each performance Major Rothwell brought on to the stage a large sack of sweets and chocolates which he then threw out to the audience. They were really intended for the children but everyone received something. Then we had to wait a whole year for the next performance, for it was an annual event.

Lilian Kellet staged many popular children's concerts in the school and she taught us action songs and dances to perform, such as 'Rendezvous', 'The Dutch Song and Dance' and 'The Sailor's Hornpipe'. Our parents made the costumes and the scenery, and much talent was displayed on the stage.

'Rendezvous' in 1934, with Betty as the shepherdess, Freda Storey as the shepherd boy and me as Cupid

Christmas was a time of magic for us, but it always seemed to me a life-time from one Christmas to the next. There were great preparations for this special time in the Tower Bank Arms. We saw mysterious parcels arriving but we never knew where they went. We had a real Christmas tree brought in from the Graythwaite Hall Estate, which Betty and I always decorated, and the house was decorated, too, with all the brass-ware on the huge mantelpiece shining like gold and everything sparkling.

On Christmas Eve the church choir came round, accompanied by Father Christmas (usually Bruce Dixon from Buckle Yeat) suitably dressed in red and with a long, white beard, singing carols at each house in the village and being invited into many of the larger houses for refreshment. I loved hearing the carols, particularly my favourites 'Away in a Manger' and 'List to the Bells'. I believe there was also a special 'Sawrey Carol'. The carol singers usually came into the Tower Bank Arms, and Father Christmas always had an orange and an apple for each of the children. The lady members of the choir were offered wine or sherry and mince pies and the men had beer and biscuits and cheese. After the choir had moved on, sandwiches, biscuits and cheese and mince pies were served in the bar, and it was then that the customers there started singing their hunting songs. In the kitchen my mother would be making rum butter, stuffing the turkey, and generally preparing for Christmas Day.

So morning came, and although it was still dark I knew that the pillow-case at the end of my bed was full. I tried to feel what the contents might be but with not having electricity in Sawrey until 1936 I had to wait until it was light enough to see. We children were not allowed to have matches to light the candle. There was usually one large present, such as a doll or a teddy bear, books, sweets and hankies and always at the bottom some new pennies, some nuts and an orange and an apple.

The Christmas story was always very vivid in my mind. Living in a village inn, I imagined that Jesus could very possibly be in our barn. Although it was used as a garage and a workshop, there was, after all, a manger in there. But then I thought to myself that my mother would certainly have brought Mary, Joseph and baby Jesus inside. Surely she would not have said there was no room. Even so I used to creep up to the barn to see if Jesus might be there, but I was always disappointed.

New Year festivities in the two Sawreys lasted for three days, with most of the events taking place in the schoolroom. On New Year's Eve there was a dance, followed by midnight service in St Peter's Church, Far Sawrey. On New Year's Day there was a wonderful party for all the children, with

Father Christmas bringing gifts for each of us. The party was followed by a concert which included singing by the choir, recitations, piano solos and duets – but not by me, as my piano playing never reached that standard. It was a real variety show. On the third day there was a whist-drive and a dance, where we took to the floor with waltzes, foxtrots, the tango and the veleta. An orchestra was always hired to play for the dancing and there were many good local orchestras then, my cousin Desmond Atkinson being the saxophonist in one of them, 'Arnold Baron's Band'.

Easter was another important festival in the village and then the place became alive with tourists, walking, bicycling or arriving by taxi or bus from Windermere Station. Every house had been spring-cleaned and the hedgerows were alive with spring flowers, primroses, celandines, buttercups, violets, bluebells, and stitchwort. The buds on the trees were just beginning to burst and the birds were heralding this wonderful queen of all seasons, spring. It was the time for the Pace-Eggers, when the Jolly Boys came round the village, portraying the characters of Lord Nelson, Jolly Jack Tar, Brown-Bags and Tosspot in the traditional mummers' play. As they acted out the play they sang the Pace-Egging Song, of which there are a number of versions. This one was written by Beatrix Potter's friend, Canon Hardwicke Rawnsley, for *Pace-Egging-Time,* a play performed by the Grasmere Players in 1906:

> Now Peggy may rest, my boys,
> And marbles may cease to be toys;
> The palm in the lane
> Is golden again
> To tell us of Easter Joys.
> The eggs at the farm
> Each morning are warm,
> To beg a few can't be wrong;
> So that I say
> Come, let's away
> To gather the eggs for our Easter play,
> And sing them the Pace-Egg Song,
> And sing them the Pace-Egg Song.
>
> Our Jack shall Nelson be,
> With ribands blue at his knee,
> With a star on his breast

16

The Jolly Boys photographed by Beatrix Potter in 1912 at Pace-Egging time

And a plume for his crest,
And a sword – a sword of the sea.
For a Jolly Jack Tar
Come fresh from the war
We will choose the best at school;
So that I say
Come let's away
To claim the eggs for our Easter play,
And keep up the Ancient Rule,
And keep up the Ancient Rule.

Now, Molly shall be Brown-Bags,
With her coat and skirt all in rags,
She has silver galore
And laid up in store,
But she's one of the miserly hags.
We will stuff a hay-sack
For a hump on his back,
And Tosspot shall have a pig-tail;

17

So that I say
Come, let's away
To gather the eggs for our Easter play,
And tell them the Old World tale,
And tell them the Old World tale.

Now, Jolly Boys all in a row,
From farm to each farm we go,
And none can resist
To go to the kist
And pay us in eggs for our show.
Red, yellow, and gold,
The eggs shall be rolled,
We will eat them three at a time;
So that I say
Come, let's away
To gather the eggs against Easter Day,
And jingle the Pace-Egg rhyme,
And jingle the Pace-Egg rhyme.

Then the Jolly Boys would collect money and pace-eggs as the reward for their performance. Our family always made pace-eggs, hard-boiling them in onion skins and sometimes painting faces on them. Two of Beatrix Potter's painted pace-eggs have been preserved and are displayed in Hill Top today.

Beatrix Potter's
painted pace-eggs

Betty and me ready
for folk-dancing

In the springtime folk-dance festivals were organised in the area and there was always a big open-air one at Grasmere. We had a folk-dance group drawn from both Sawreys, of which William Heelis was a member. He was also an expert Morris dancer. Beatrix Potter paid for the material for the ladies' dresses, and the group really stood out at the festivals, with the men in white flannel trousers and white shirts, and the ladies in their dresses of a lovely pink material patterned with roses. Beatrix Potter did not dance but she occasionally attended the meetings just to watch and to draw. What a wonderful time we had.

> Listen! Come listen!
> What joy, what pleasure,
> The band is playing our favourite tune.
> Let us dance, let us sing,
> And spin and twirl as we did when young.
> 'Rufty Tufty', 'Strip the Willow', 'Newcastle'.
> Take your partners, form a circle,
> The band is playing 'Circassian Circle'.
> Moonlight and music in plentiful measure,
> Brings back fond memories lasting for ever.

The sun always seemed to be shining on May Day, everything and everybody looked beautiful. The May Queen was usually the eldest girl in that particular year, so I was never chosen, but at the crowning of the May Queen we all danced round the maypole. I loved plaiting the ribbons and some of the designs were quite intricate. The children wore crowns of real flowers and pretty dresses, and there was apple blossom everywhere. They were indeed happy times.

Continuing the village tradition, Hazel Byers crowned Dorothy Walker as the May Queen in 1954

Many of the women in the village, adults and children, belonged to The Girls Friendly Society (GFS), an organisation which was set up nation-wide in the First World War but which no longer exists. The objects of the Society were 'to unite for the Glory of God, in one Fellowship of prayer and service, the girls and women of the Empire, to uphold purity in thought, word and deed'. There were about six girls in my age group and we used to meet at Low House, one of the oldest cottages in Near Sawrey, and at Sunnyside, Miss Jones's home.

At the age of eleven, any pupil in Sawrey School, or one of the surrounding village schools, could sit for a Sandys Scholarship, named after the Sandys family of Hawkshead. If they passed, the scholarship would provide the money to enable the pupil to go to the Grammar School in Ambleside or Ulverston, for secondary education was not free until 1944. Children who failed the exam stayed on at their village schools until they were fourteen, when they left to find work – often as apprentices.

I was lucky enough to pass the exam and I have to admit that I was glad to leave Miss Jones behind when I moved on to the Kelsick Grammar School in Ambleside. Compared with the secondary schools of today Kelsick Grammar was small, but to me, after the Sawrey school, it seemed very grand, another world. To get there I had to bicycle from Near Sawrey to Hawkshead (two miles) to catch Jim Airey's bus to Ambleside, and then walk half-way up Wansfell to beyond the Stock Ghyll Falls, so I had plenty of exercise.

Every Speech Day we sang our school song of which we were all very proud. This is the first verse:

> John Kelsick was a gentleman of substance and renown,
> He built a school in Ambleside to educate the town.
> 'Tis now this school we're proud to call,
> Our school whose praise we're singing.
> So raise your voices one and all, and set the rafters ringing.
> Success attend our Kelsick school, and all its scholars clever.
> Come boys and girls with one accord
> Shout Kelsick School for ever.

The Sandys Scholarship was administered by the Hawkshead solicitors, W.H. Heelis & Son. William Heelis was Beatrix Potter's husband and they had met when he was negotiating the purchase of Hill Top Farm for her in 1905. They had married in 1913 and chosen Castle Cottage in Near Sawrey as their home, for Beatrix Potter had never lived in the house at Hill Top Farm, just coming to stay there when she could snatch some time away from her parents in London.

William Heelis was a real gentleman and very much respected in the area. He must have told his wife who the lucky children were to have gained a scholarship, for when she learned that I was one of them, I was no longer the 'naughty little girl' and she continued to show interest in my progress at school.

Beatrix Potter was always willing to lend articles as 'props' for the school plays but, as far as I know, she never visited the school, although in 1935, to mark the Silver Jubilee of King George V and Queen Mary, she presented it with a John Peel Jug. Only a few of these jugs were produced and each one contained a wind-up mechanism which played the tune of 'John Peel'. The jug was used as a sports trophy and when the school closed in the 1960s it was given to the church. However, as there was nowhere to display it, the jug was handed over to the National Trust on permanent loan to be included in the collection at Hill Top.

Betty with the John Peel Jug presented to Sawrey School by Beatrix Potter in 1935. Geoff Storey is in the middle of the back row

Beatrix Potter as I remember her

Beatrix Potter was a curious mixture, always a Victorian, wearing long tweed skirts and jackets made from her own Herdwick sheep's wool. She wore an old felt hat in winter and a straw hat in summer. We never saw her in a light dress, even in very hot weather. She had her clogs made by a local shoemaker in Hawkshead, Charlie Brown, and today his little shoe shop is an attractive café, The Old Cobbler's Tea-Shop, much frequented by locals and tourists to sample the home-baked fare. When it was raining Beatrix Potter threw an old sack around her shoulders printed with the name 'BIBBY'S', the firm which produced animal feeds. One wet day, walking between Near and Far Sawrey, she was mistaken for a tramp.

One prominent family in the area was the Edmondson family who lived in a large mansion called Bryerswood, at the top of Ferry Hill, overlooking Windermere. They were very generous to the village school and gave several books as prizes each year. In 1929 Miss Norah Edmondson wrote a delightful book for children called *The Lavender Garden,* for which Beatrix Potter wrote the preface and, it is now believed, also contributed the drawing of violets for the contents page.

Haytime in Sawrey was a real fun-time for children. It was wonderful, it was magic, how we loved it. The farmer first scythed the edges of each field before the main part was cut with horse and mower and, after the hay had been gathered in, we children were allowed to rake up the bits that were left. Those glorious, hot, summer days, riding on the hay carts, playing hide-and-seek behind the haystacks, sharing a picnic tea with the farmers in the hay fields – all the farmers except Beatrix Potter that is. Most of us were never allowed into her fields. There was only one child who could go into her hay field and that was Geoff Storey, the son of her shepherd, Tom Storey. Even Tom's daughter, Freda, could never join in the fun of haytime. On one occasion Freda took a message to her father and was promptly told by Beatrix Potter to go home and to put on a longer dress – and to keep out of the hay field.

Tom Storey and his family had moved to Hill Top Farm in 1928. His wife, Hilda (*née* Stables), was my mother's second cousin, and they were great friends. When they killed a pig at the farm, Hilda would always bring my mother black puddings, spare-ribs, pig's trotters and other bits and pieces from the pig. In the autumn she would bring apples, turnips and all kinds of fruit and vegetables which had been harvested. She was an extremely kind woman. However, she had to wait for a convenient moment when 'the boss' was not around, for she never dared to let her know she was giving things away from the farm. While Beatrix Potter would not have wanted to keep the produce for herself, being an astute business woman she would have sold it. Her generosity was centred on the National Trust and through that organisation on the preservation of the Lake District.

The Storeys had little privacy while they were living at Hill Top Farm, for there was a connecting door into Beatrix Potter's part of the house from their farm kitchen. Hilda Storey was very deaf, and many a time while she was going about her work she would turn round and discover with some shock that Beatrix Potter was standing there behind her. I presume the mistress of the house felt that she could come and go as she wished. It was, after all, her farm and the Storeys were her employees.

It is my belief that Beatrix Potter truly did not understand children. I doubt whether she had ever played a child's game in her life, because she had no childhood friends. People say to me, 'How can you say that, when she wrote those beautiful stories for children?' I agree; they are lovely stories and are beautifully illustrated, but those stories were filling the gap in her own childhood. There is no doubt, though, that she was a genius, a multi-talented woman. Lady Ulla Hyde Parker, in her book *Cousin Beatie*, described her in this way:

> [She] had a presence which commanded respect. She had the self-assurance of a person who is aware of the qualities within herself, however little the world might be aware of them, and who also knows what values she upholds and stands for. Perhaps such qualities are found only in people who have suffered for their strong individuality, in people who cannot be 'shaped', since some inner compass needles constantly seem to swing back to the point of direction they have to follow.

As children we never thought of Beatrix Potter as a famous author and artist. She was simply Mrs Heelis, a farmer and villager, and someone to be wary of. We were able to buy her little books from the village shop, which she portrayed in *The Tale of Ginger and Pickles* (though on the jacket of the book she gave it a bow window which it never had, *see below*).

Owned by old Bob Taylor and his wife, the shop sold everything from a packet of pins to a sack of potatoes and it had a unique smell, a mixture of herbs, soap, bacon and candles all rolled into one. There were glass jars on the counter full of sweets, humbugs, toffees, pear drops, mintoes, and it was fascinating to watch Mrs Taylor roll a sheet of paper into a cone shaped bag to put them in. Every birthday my father would take me down to the shop to buy one of the little books (one shilling and sixpence then – £4.50 now) and some chocolates. Unfortunately, none of my original copies of the books have survived; they were too well thumbed through.

Me aged about 8 with Belle outside the village shop

Mrs Bob Taylor's niece, Dorothy Swift, came to live with her aunt and to help in the shop. One day Beatrix Potter called in to speak to Mrs Taylor.

'Are you aware that your niece is walking out with young William Postlethwaite?' she said.

'I certainly am,' Mrs Taylor replied.

'And do you approve?'

'Of course I do, he's a nice young man and a hard worker,' said Mrs Taylor, who was really very annoyed that this woman should be meddling in something that was none of her business.

Beatrix Potter frequently made herself unpopular with the villagers by interfering in their lives. When she heard that my sister was going to marry a Londoner, she was most concerned, saying to my mother, 'I do hope he is worthy of such a lovely girl!' You could detect something of her mother, old Mrs Potter, in that remark. *She* had never thought anybody was suitable for her own daughter, Beatrix.

Opposite what was the old shop is Anvil Cottage where Mollie Green (*née* Byers) lived. Mollie was born in Oak Cottage, in the nearby village of Cunsey, on 4 May 1903, the younger sister of Harry Byers, who would be for many years gardener to Beatrix Potter. The children's maternal grandfather, Joseph Strickland, was the ferryman, and their father, Jack, had been a partner in a grocery business at a corner shop in Far Sawrey. When he died Harry, being the eldest, became the breadwinner. Mollie's mother, Mrs Byers, was what we call in this part of the world the confectioner, baking bread, cakes, scones, tea-cakes and pies. Mollie was known by everyone as 'Mollie Muffins' and every Friday she went round to all the cottages in the village with a large market basket on her arm full of goodies for sale. Beatrix Potter always bought two delicious pork pies, one for herself and one for her husband, Willie Heelis.

In 1936, when Mollie's mother was very ill, Beatrix Potter went to Bruce Dixon, who had the timber yard immediately opposite Anvil Cottage, and asked him if he would oblige by not using the saw, as it made such a dreadful noise and was causing much stress to Mrs Byers. Beatrix Potter wanted her to die in peace.

Left alone in Anvil Cottage, Mollie Byers occupied herself with the 'Bed and Breakfasts' and 'Teas and Coffees' for the tourists. It was just the kind of place where groups of bicyclists and tricyclists used to call for refreshment, particularly those from Yorkshire, and one of the men began to call more often than the rest. Charles Edmund Green (Ed), a representative for Rowntrees of York, made Anvil Cottage his regular

Mollie Green taking delivery of her paper from Gladys Dobson in the porch of Anvil Cottage

stopping place whenever he was in the area, and in 1939 he and Mollie were married in St Peter's Church, Far Sawrey, leaving for their honeymoon on a tandem. On their return, the Greens lived at Anvil Cottage and Mollie continued with her baking and her teas.

Next door to the shop was the Smithy where Fred Satterthwaite and George Devon shoed the horses. When I was a child, shire horses were used on all the farms and in the timber trade. They were magnificent animals and it was not until after the Second World War that tractors replaced them in this area.

Fred Satterthwaite and George Devon at the Smithy

Beatrix Potter would often stop and have a chat with Fred as she was passing. On one occasion, Fred was telling her about the new cooking range he had installed in his kitchen at home and suggested that perhaps she ought to have one at Castle Cottage. She very curtly told him that she had a perfectly good range on which her housekeeper Mary Rogerson cooked excellent meals. She wanted nothing to do with these new-fangled things.

Fred's house, Belle Green, was just up the lane from the Smithy in Market Street, so called because it was the centre of village trading. Beatrix Potter had stayed at Belle Green with the Satterthwaites in 1906 while the extension was built on to Hill Top for the Cannon family, who were living in the old farmhouse and managing the farm. They had been asked to stay on when she bought Hill Top, but she wanted to have the original house for her own use on her visits from London. Fred Satterthwaite had a dear little dog called Mettle and Beatrix Potter put it into her last book, *The Fairy Caravan.*

On the upper side of the Smithy was the carpenter's shop where Billy Kenyon, nephew of Bob Taylor, was both undertaker and carpenter. The smell of newly-sawn timber, sawdust and wood-shavings always brings back memories to me of that carpenter's shop. We collected all sorts of bits and pieces from there to use in our 'baby-house' – a little place we created in a corner of the orchard under an old yew tree at Buckle Yeat, the home of Duchess in *The Tale of the Pie and the Patty-Pan.*

My school friend, Margaret Dixon, lived at Buckle Yeat and it was her father who was the timber merchant. Margaret and I had so much fun creating wonderful games. We picked wild flowers and wild strawberries,

Me on my tricycle, with my friends
Margaret and Eileen Dixon

we collected tadpoles and watched them grow into frogs in large glass jars at school. We collected conkers (horse-chestnuts) and mushrooms and we often went apple scrumping in Beatrix Potter's orchard adjoining the timber yard. She knew we went in there and she also knew it was an overwhelming temptation for small children, so she tied a ribbon round one of the trees and told us we could only pick apples from that tree. But they were not the best apples, not so sweet and juicy as our favourites called 'Tom Thumb', so I am afraid we still managed to take one or two apples from the other trees.

Next door to this orchard is Sawrey House, a large residence with a wide expanse of garden, overlooking Esthwaite Water. Two of my childhood friends lived there, Devoke and Whillan Spence, the daughters of Kenneth and Gwen Spence. Kenneth Spence was one of the founders of The Friends of the Lake District and he also initiated the Youth Hostels Association in this area. Although he was promoting very similar aims to Beatrix Potter, both of them working for the conservation and preservation of the Lake District, the two were at daggers drawn for some unknown reason.

In the summertime, Devoke, Whillan and myself used to run around wearing just a pair of shorts, but Beatrix Potter could not bear to see us like this. She would get really angry and say, 'Get yourselves home and put on some clothes. You can't go round the village like that!', waving her shepherd's crook threateningly at us. I just wonder what her reaction would be if she were to come back and experience life in the modern world?

The village Post Office was situated down the lane alongside the Meadow. It was owned by George and Lizzy May Garnett. She was the post-mistress and he had a barn-cum-workshop where he repaired bicycles and charged wireless batteries. Lizzy May's mother lived with them and she was a frightening figure, rather like a witch. The passages in the old Post Office were dark and menacing and I used to hate having to go there for stamps and postal orders, because this witch-like figure would appear in the dim-lit passage. Not that she ever spoke, but it was her appearance which made you want to turn and run out of the place, and I was always glad to see Lizzy May appear. Lizzy May and her mother died on the same day, I would think of malnourishment. Theirs was the first double funeral in the village and it was a very sad occasion.

Beatrix Potter then bought the old Post Office, together with the adjoining cottage and the old barn. She housed her chauffeur, Walter Stevens and his

My friend, Whillan Spence, *c.*1927, in the doorway of the old Post Office, which appears as Mrs Ribby's house in *The Tale of the Pie and the Patty-Pan.*

wife, in the old Post Office and converted the barn into an attractive cottage. George Garnett went to live in a caravan next to Garth Cottage, where there was a barn in which he could carry on his cycle-repair work and battery charging. He was one of the eccentric characters in the village, and there were a few in the area, I might add.

There was old Miss Grafton who lived in Cunsey. She was a very strange lady who kept Clumber spaniels, and lived in a large house called Fellborough on the shores of Windermere, hidden from passers-by by a high wall. She celebrated each of the dogs' birthdays with a cake made by Mollie Green, on which was written 'Happy Birthday to _____', whatever the dog's name was. When the dogs died they were each given a proper burial in the garden at Fellborough, with a headstone inscribed with their name. These dogs were her children, she adored them. As she was nearing the end of her life and had just one remaining dog, she dressed in the uniform of a nanny and took the dog for walks in a push-chair. When she died Miss Grafton left everything she had to a dogs' home – and to the polar bears in Chester Zoo.

William Postlethwaite kept the farm called High Green Gate, opposite the Smithy in Market Street. He had a large family, and his two sons worked with him on the farm. Mary, one of his daughters, worked in the farmhouse with her mother. Beatrix Potter and William Postlethwaite were always arguing about something or other. As they sat in the porch at High Green Gate arguing, Mrs Postlethwaite could hear them from inside and would become quite embarrassed. William told Beatrix she ought to go and live on an island away from everybody. When Beatrix told him he might feature in one of her books, he objected strongly. 'You had better not put me into one of your damned silly books.' But she did, and here he is, as Farmer Potatoes in *The Tale of Samuel Whiskers* or *The Roly-Poly Pudding*.

When Amanda Postlethwaite, William's youngest daughter, married Bob Thistlethwaite – quite a combination of surnames – Beatrix Potter knocked on her door and handed her an envelope, saying, 'Mr Heelis asked me to give you this.' Inside was a cheque for £2, Amanda's wedding gift. That was a reasonable amount for a wedding gift in those days but from someone whom we knew to be as rich as Beatrix Potter it seemed rather small. As the cheque was signed 'Beatrix Potter', Amanda now wishes she had kept it and had it framed.

When electricity at last came to Sawrey in 1936, it was brought from Troutbeck Bridge by underground cable, laid on the bed of Windermere and in trenches dug along the roadside up to the village. When the operation was complete, there were great celebrations for the switch-on, with a spectacular ball in the Sawrey Hotel at Far Sawrey, at that time tenanted by Miss Elizabeth Robinson and her sister, Mabel. The entire village was lit up, except Hill Top and Castle Cottage, for Beatrix Potter refused to have electricity in her houses. 'But you can put it in the byres; the cows might like it,' she said.

I had two aunts, Millie and Lena, living in the south of England, not far from London, and during my long summer holidays from school I went to visit them in Cockfosters and in Hornchurch. It was a great adventure for me because it was a long, overnight train journey from Windermere. New clothes were packed at least a week before, and then unpacked and re-packed several times to make sure everything was in order. My mother 'delivered' me to London, and one of our relatives usually brought me home. We left Windermere Station at 8.30 p.m. and arrived in Euston at about 6.30 the following morning. I always tried very hard to stay awake all night but I never succeeded. Then there was the journey on the Underground to whichever aunt I was staying with.

I was taken to all the famous places in London. One of the highlights, I remember, was waving to the little Princesses at their home, 145 Piccadilly. When the family were in residence, Princess Elizabeth and Princess Margaret Rose would often be at the window of their nursery watching passers-by, and it was a great thrill when they waved to the public. They were the prettiest little girls.

Dining in London restaurants was a special treat, particularly when there was an orchestra playing. Theatre visits were always exciting and quite spectacular to a small girl from the country dazzled by the grandeur of the decor and beguiled by the ice cream in the interval. When I returned home

With my aunts, Millie and Cissie, and my cousin, Desmond, on holiday in Hornchurch

from my holidays, I was usually determined that I would be an actress and live in London. How glad I am that ambition was never fulfilled!

Outings from the village school were invariably to a local seaside town, Grange, Morecambe, Walney Island or Bardsea, where we would spend our pocket money within the first hour and eat our picnic lunch much too early. But we always had an enjoyable day and we sang loudly all the way home in the coach, which was called a charabanc then. Outings from the Grammar School were trips by rail to the big cities, Edinburgh, Glasgow, Liverpool, Manchester or Chester, leaving very early in the morning and arriving home very late with bulging files of notes and information on the local museum or factory we had visited.

I was a Brownie from the age of seven, then went on to be a Girl Guide. Our meetings were held in Hawkshead, Brownies in the old Grammar School and Guides in the Quaker Meeting House at Colthouse. Our Brown Owl was Wynne Heelis, wife of William Heelis's nephew and partner, Jack. One year our Brownie meetings were held in Hill Top, where Wynne and Jack were living while their house was being built in Hawkshead.

Beatrix Potter always encouraged and supported the Guide movement. She allowed Guide companies from the cities to camp in Bull Banks in Near Sawrey (the home of her characters Mr Tod and Tommy Brock from *The Tale of Mr Tod*) and we looked forward every year to their arrival

The Guides fetch water for their camp at Bull Banks

because they let us join in their games, their treasure hunts and daily activities. On arrival the Guides would all go over to Hill Top Farm to fill their palliasses with hay or straw, and to pick up some milk. Their camp-fires were great fun, lit as dusk was falling, and we sat round the fire singing favourite camp-fire songs, eating huge chunks of bread and jam and drinking hot cocoa. Occasionally Beatrix Potter would come to the camp-fires but she always sat apart from the rest of us, for she never seemed comfortable in a group. She obviously enjoyed listening to the songs, though, and often when the locals were having a sing-song in the bar of the Tower Bank Arms, she would walk up and down on the opposite side of the road listening to the hunting songs.

However, she was not always pleased to encourage her admirers. One year we had two student teachers staying at the Tower Bank Arms who were anxious to meet her, and they decided they would just walk up to Hill Top and knock on her door. On the way up the flag path they met an old woman who asked them what they were looking for. They told her they were hoping to find Beatrix Potter at home.

'I am she,' said Beatrix. 'What is your business?'

'Well, we are student teachers,' replied the girls. 'We read your little books to our children in school and we wanted to meet and talk with you.'

'You would do more good teaching the little brats some manners,' said Beatrix, abruptly, 'Never mind reading them those silly books.'

The poor girls were flabbergasted. At a loss to know how to answer, they simply turned round and came away. Beatrix Potter never sought fame or publicity and she was never happy about people seeking her out without warning.

Guests staying at the Tower Bank Arms would often ask about the old woman who walked past almost every day. When my mother told them it was Beatrix Potter, the children's author, they could hardly believe her, and it took much explaining to convince them. But I think Beatrix Potter was amused to think that people didn't recognise her, she liked to be incognito. She came to live in the Lake District because she loved the countryside and the country way of life, she wanted to be a country woman and to cast off all signs of her city upbringing. She liked a simple way of life, no pomp and no circumstance. I am sure that the thirty years she was married to William Heelis were the happiest years of her life, content in her surroundings and successful in her achievements. She was truly a great lady.

Beatrix Potter's housekeeper was called Mary Rogerson, but there were two Mary Rogersons in Near Sawrey, which sometimes led to confusion.

Mary Rogerson and Sally Benson with Beatrix Potter's dogs outside Castle Cottage

My father's mother's sister, my great-aunt, was Mary Rogerson (*née* Atkinson) senior. She bred Pomeranian dogs, and it was her little white dog, Duchess, who became the little black dog in *The Tale of the Pie and the Patty-Pan*. When Mary Allonby married her son, she too became Mary Rogerson – Beatrix Potter's housekeeper. Helping her in the house was Sally Benson, and in Beatrix Potter's story *Wag-by-Wall* (published in America by The Horn Book Inc., Boston), the main character is called Sally Benson, based, I am sure, on our Sally. The real Sally Benson, however, did not live in a thatched cottage, for there were no thatched cottages in Sawrey, all the roofs in the area being of slate from the local quarries. Beatrix Potter owned several quarries which came with her farms, and she gave the stone from one of them to build Ees Bridge near Esthwaite Water, just down the hill from Pigling Bland's crossroads, close to where some say Mr. Jeremy Fisher lived.

One property to which Beatrix Potter was much attracted but never owned was Townend in Troutbeck. My mother was a descendant of the Browne family of Townend and my father of the Atkinson family of Sawrey, both very ancient Lakeland families. My father's mother was an Atkinson but I never knew her because she had died when my father was seven. He was brought up by aunts and uncles and was put to work on a farm when he was only a young boy. He had a hard life, joining the army, The Border Regiment, when the First World War broke out. His father, Edward Burns, remarried and he was someone I never really liked when I was a child. When we visited him he was always sitting in an armchair by the fire filling his pipe with Black Twist, a tobacco sold in lengths which had to be cut into pieces with a knife. He would roll a piece round and round in his hands before pressing it into his pipe and then he would suck the pipe when he was lighting up. It was quite a ritual but I thought it a dirty habit – and the smell was awful.

I have information about the Brownes dating back to the early sixteenth century, probably earlier. My great-grandfather, John Browne, who died in 1883, was the uncle of the last George Browne to live in Townend. John Browne farmed at Moor Farm, in Torver, near Coniston, and his name is inscribed above the Torver school door. He had two sons and three daughters and the only one to marry was my grandmother, Dora Jane Browne. Her life is a singular story in itself but, briefly, her first husband,

My maternal grandmother, Dora Jane Browne

Ben Casson, died young, an alcoholic. Her second husband, William Rawes, also died young, of pneumonia but fond of his alcohol, too. There were five daughters from that marriage, the youngest dying when she was only two years old. My mother, Margaret Browne Rawes, was the middle daughter and she married William Edward Burns in 1918 at the end of the First World War.

George Browne had three daughters, and I remember visiting old Aunt Clara, the last of them, at Townend on many occasions with my mother. It has changed very little if at all since then. Beatrix Potter went to Townend regularly. She and Aunt Clara were the same age and they died in the same year, 1943. Similar in type, they both retained their Victorian habits and their belief that children should be seen but not heard. Beatrix Potter used to tell my mother how she would love to own Townend, so she would be happy to know that today it belongs to the National Trust and receives about 25,000 visitors a year.

My mother, Margaret (*top right*), with her sisters Cissie, Lena and Millie, *c.*1907

2.

AT THE CROSSROADS

On 21 January 1936 the nation went into mourning. King George V had died in Sandringham House and now Edward, Prince of Wales, had become King Edward VIII. I was thirteen years old and I well remember the concern there was amongst the people as to what sort of King he would make. Edward, known by everyone as David, had been a popular figure as Prince of Wales, but he had modern ideas and was very much his own man. What was more, his name was linked with that of Mrs Ernest Simpson, the American divorcée; as he was head of the Church of England, she was someone he could never marry. When, finally, he made his decision to renounce the throne so he could be with her, he made a very moving speech which we all listened to on the radio. 'I have found it impossible to carry the heavy burden of responsibility and to discharge my duties as King as I would wish to do without the help and support of the woman I love.'

So ended one of the shortest reigns in English history. Until then history lessons at school had been dull and uninteresting, full only of dates and place names, but now history was being made before my own eyes. On 12 May, 1937, the new King, George VI, was crowned in Westminster Abbey, but during the period of shock over the Abdication and the joyous celebrations for the Coronation, the threat of war was hanging over us.

I was still at school when the Second World War was declared and one of my aunts and her family had already sought refuge from London in the Tower Bank Arms. I remember that fateful day, 3 September 1939, so well. At 11 a.m. we all listened to Neville Chamberlain's speech on the radio. My mother and my aunt, who could both remember the First World War so vividly, were crying, but apart from that there was a grim silence in the house, which continued for the rest of the day, or so it seemed.

Grizedale Hall, in the Grizedale Forest, three miles from Hawkshead on the way to Satterthwaite, had been designated for use as a prisoner-of-war camp and army vehicles and personnel were already moving through Near Sawrey. Gas masks, identity cards and ration books had been issued to everyone, the Home Guard was formed and more fire-fighters were recruited. Groups of pacifists and Irishmen were billeted in empty houses in the village and went to work in the forests, replacing our young men who had been called up for war service. The whole area seemed to change overnight.

I was busy studying for my School Certificate and Matriculation, and my sister Betty was helping out at home. The village shop had closed, High

Green Gate was no longer a farmhouse but a guest house. Evacuees from the cities were pouring into the countryside, hoping it would be a safe haven, which it was, except when the Luftwaffe bombed the Barrow shipyards and dropped their stray bombs on their return journey. When this happened, the animals were at risk, too. As Beatrix Potter wrote to an American friend:

> I had 2 horses in a field next to a pasture where 11 bombs dropped and my man found them grazing quietly when daylight came. We thought those bombs were dropped because the German suddenly realized that he was heading straight into the fell side in the darkness. They were only small bombs; it is interesting to look at the holes amongst the turf & rushes.

I left school in July 1940, having passed my exams, I am glad to say, with distinction, and I remember crying all day. My time at school had been so happy that I never wanted my school days to end. When I tell my grandchildren about it, they think I am crazy. 'Imagine not wanting to leave school!' they exclaim.

The next few months were a time of love and romance – and of finding a niche in the outside world. It was suggested that a career in accountancy might be suitable for me, maths having been my strong subject at school, and it just so happened that my mother knew Edward Tyson, the accountant in Ambleside. Before long I found myself cycling to Ambleside again every day and working in a miserable, dingy office behind the Midland Bank, opposite the White Lion Hotel, earning eight shillings and sixpence a week. I was also doing a postal course in accountancy.

Edward Tyson himself was away on active service in the Royal Air Force, so he employed a chartered accountant, a Mr James, who lived with his wife in a flat above the office, happy to be in the Lake District away from all the bombing in London. Mr James used to give me a lot of advice, and one particular piece I remember well. 'Never marry a man who earns less than five pounds a week. When poverty walks in at the front door, love walks out at the back!'

Mr James was truly concerned about my welfare. Perhaps he thought I was a vulnerable little country girl, capable of being tempted by the wrong type?

At home, soldiers guarding the Grizedale prisoner-of-war camp came to the Tower Bank Arms in the evenings when they were off duty. In those days the bar closed at 10 p.m. and often some of them would stay and chat with my father. My mother, being the kind person she was, would provide

Me in my school uniform, with my family and some guests outside the
Tower Bank Arms

Jim Taylor in 1941, soon after
we met

them with a plate of sandwiches or biscuits and cheese, knowing that they had the long walk of some four miles back to camp. One of these soldiers stood apart from the rest. Tall, good-looking and a real gentleman, Signalman Jim Taylor had been brought to Grizedale by his friend Colonel Cobb, the commandant of the camp, to be his batman. He had come straight from Dunkirk, one of the lucky ones to get back to England.

Jim was a keen ballroom dancer, as I was, and almost every Friday and Saturday when he was not on duty he would come to the dances held in one or other of the village halls in the district. He had a great sense of humour and we enjoyed being together. One night at the Tower Bank Arms he disappeared to have a long talk with my mother.

'I'm afraid I have fallen in love with your daughter, Willow,' he told her. 'I know there is a big age gap between us – after all, I am thirty-three and she is only seventeen – but do you mind if I take her to the pictures and to dances?'

So it was agreed that Jim and I could spend time together when Jim was off duty and when I was not studying.

Freda Storey and me setting off to
do the shopping in Bowness

I was starting to grow tired of being shut up in that dark accountancy office all day, adding up long columns of figures while the sun shone from a brilliant blue sky, but when I told my mother that I wanted to leave, she was not at all pleased. 'I hope you are not going to be someone who flits from job to job. You will have to settle down in one place at some time.'

It so happened that the Provincial Insurance Company was advertising for school leavers to train in their Kendal office, and the wage they were offering was about twenty-five shillings a week, three times as much as I was earning from Mr Tyson. It was agreed that I should go for an interview and, to my delight, I was accepted. I now cycled to Windermere each day, crossing by the ferry, and caught the bus to Kendal. If I missed the bus for any reason, I could always catch the train.

It was at this time that Franz Von Werra, the German fighter pilot, escaped from Grizedale Hall, only ten days after his arrival there. Every two days, twenty-four prisoners were taken out on the road for exercise, accompanied by a sergeant mounted on a horse, and an officer with four guards in the front of the column and four at the rear. On this particular day, after two miles they rested by a low stone wall, and while the guards bought apples from a passing greengrocer's cart, Von Werra escaped over the wall. When it was discovered that he was missing, the Home Guard, the local police and three bloodhounds started the hunt for him in the pouring rain.

After three days and nights everyone began to lose hope that the escaped prisoner would be found, but on the fourth day two members of the Home Guard, patrolling the Broughton Mills area, found him hiding in a hut. However, once again he managed to get away and he was not found until two days later, when a shepherd spotted him on a hill overlooking the Duddon Valley. The Cumberland and Westmorland Constabulary were called out and Von Werra was finally recaptured. He was put into solitary confinement in the camp for twenty-one days and then sent to Swanwick, a prisoner-of-war camp in the Midlands.

When I wasn't at the Provincial Insurance Company, I was an enthusiastic member of the Sawrey Amateur Dramatic Society, and later of the Hawkshead Stage Society. I loved amateur dramatics. We entered one-act plays in the district drama festivals and on several occasions we won a shield or a cup. I could hardly believe it when I was awarded the first bursary in the area to attend a drama summer school in Oxford, held at Lady Margaret Hall. While I was there, and enjoying every minute, I regretted that but for the war and my very strict parents, my education might have continued at college or university. My life would have taken a very different course.

Then, through the door, came my call-up papers. I was now eighteen and deemed old enough to fight for my king and country. I was delighted, for I very much wanted to join the Women's Royal Air Force, but my mother had other plans. She knew that there were Land Girls employed on the nearby Graythwaite Hall Estate. If I went there she would be able to keep a watchful eye on me. So the Land Army it had to be, but I must admit that I loved it. Working outside all day in the fields and forests was the perfect job for me; such a happy release from a stuffy, centrally-heated office in Kendal. What was more, I was paid three pounds a week for a job I really enjoyed. We felled small trees in coppices, did fencing, bundled pea-sticks and peeled pit-props for the coal mines. We carted these down to Lakeside Station on George Stewardson's wagon. We also helped at haytime, and with gardening and general estate work. In our uniforms of cream shirts and green pullovers, knee breeches and long socks, we worked hard from 7.30 a.m. to 5 p.m., except during haytime when we sometimes did not finish until after ten in the evening.

In August of 1941 my sister married John Cockman, a Londoner who had first come to the Lake District on holiday with a friend, staying at the Tower Bank Arms. After meeting Betty, John started writing to her and then he kept coming back. When Beatrix Potter heard that they were getting married, she

(*Right*) In my Land Girl's working
uniform in the porch at Hill Top
(*Below*) Carting pit-props on George
Stewardson's wagon

gave Betty all her clothing coupons, claiming that she had no use for them herself. In the middle of that year Colonel Cobb and Jim had been transferred to Catterick in Yorkshire. Fortunately Jim had a motor-bike, so he was able to come over to Sawrey to see me whenever he could.

In the north of England, we always keep the Scottish tradition of first-footing on New Year's Eve, when the first person to enter your home after midnight is supposed to be a dark-haired male, carrying a piece of coal and a bottle of whisky. On New Year's Eve in 1941, Jim and I went out of the back door of the Tower Bank Arms and round to the coal-house to fetch a piece of coal. Jim had the whisky bottle in his pocket, but he also had a small box containing a diamond ring, which he placed on my finger. So we were engaged in the coal-house – and went back inside through the front door on New Year's Day, for you must never enter through the same door as you left by when first-footing. Two months later, on 28 February 1942, we were married in St Peter's Church in Far Sawrey and spent our three-day honeymoon in the snow at the Scafell Hotel in Borrowdale, near Keswick.

I returned to the Tower Bank Arms, as Jim was now stationed in Dumfries where his unit was preparing to be shipped off to North Africa, and I would not see him again until the end of the war. Almost immediately doubts began to surface in my mind. Should we have married? Did we really know each other? He was sixteen years older than I – and I was only nineteen. All I could do now was to wait and to hope that I had done the right thing. Some months later I wrote the following poem which I called 'Moments of Reflection':

When the dawn breaks in the sky,
The mist rises from the lakes,
The birds herald in a new day,
And the whole of creation awakes.

I am alone with my thoughts,
Recollecting happy times.
Together we strolled down country lanes.
Wandered through woods carpeted with bluebells,
Sat by the lake shore
Watching a family of swans sail by
To who knows where?
We were so happy then, and very much in love.

Our wedding, on a snowy day, 28 February 1942

Visions appear of those wonderful bygone days,
Meeting in the moonlight, dancing at the ball.
Stealing a forbidden kiss,
I was too young – or so I was told!

O Lord, please let there be Peace,
May all wars cease.
Bring him home, please bring him home.
I pray that we will be together again.
God's blessings are immeasurable.

Listening to news of the war on the radio, we all realised how fortunate we were to be living in a beautiful village, far from the horrors of air raids and the devastation of the cities. My family was never short of a nourishing meal, as the pub customers brought us rabbits, pheasants, venison and wood pigeons. Our sugar ration we gave up to our father.

We all had to wait a long time for news from our husbands and sons who were right up there in the front line, and while we waited we kept busy with war work, knitting socks, balaclava helmets, gloves and sweaters for the troops, working on the farms and in the forests. We were also raising money for good causes and putting on shows in both Sawreys and in Hawkshead.

Peter Hoggarth as Winston Churchill in the fancy dress parade at the
'Wings for Victory' garden fête, June 1943

My bicycle, patriotically decorated in red, white and blue for the June 1943 fête

A whole week of events was held in Near and Far Sawrey at the beginning of June 1943 to raise money for a country-wide campaign called 'Wings for Victory', opening with a garden fête at Sawrey Knotts, the home of Mr and Mrs Hack at the top of Ferry Hill. Their garden was in full bloom and the view from it over Windermere was truly magnificent. There were several competitions, a fancy dress parade, a treasure hunt, and a dressed-up bicycle parade. I was so proud of my bicycle which was decked out in red, white and blue! The target for our campaign was set at £2,500, but we more than doubled it, thanks to the generosity of the villagers.

In December of that year Beatrix Potter died. From 1939 to the time of her death she had been in the Royal Women's Hospital in Liverpool on three separate occasions, and had undergone some serious operations. It was obvious to us all that her health was failing but, in spite of that, and being the stalwart that she was, her interest in and enthusiasm for her farms and her love for the little Herdwick sheep never waned.

On the evening of 21 December 1943 she sent for her shepherd, Tom Storey, to come to Castle Cottage. Very near the end of her life, she was still able to give Tom his final instructions on the disposal of her ashes,

Beatrix Potter, Mrs William Heelis

which had to be kept a close secret. Tom knew that he would not see her again after that. He told us, 'By gum, she was a good boss. I couldn't have had a better. I knew she was at peace, I could see it in her bonny face.'

The following evening, 22 December 1943, Beatrix Potter died at home in Castle Cottage, leaving behind a rich legacy for the whole world – her writings, her drawings, her farms and cottages, over 4,000 acres of land, her flocks of Herdwick sheep, and much more.

It was a very sad time in the village and we all felt her loss. Even though she never really mixed in with village life, she had always been a central character

William Heelis

because we saw her almost every day. Poor Mr Heelis looked a sad and lonely figure. Mary Rogerson continued to look after him in Castle Cottage, as did his good neighbours, Miss Mills and Miss Hammond, who had lived next door since 1922.

When someone in the village community died, it was the normal practice at that time for local people to draw their curtains while the coffin was brought through the village to the church, but there was no service in church for Mrs Heelis. She was taken to the crematorium at Blackpool and cremated there on 31 December.

On New Year's Day, just as the Storeys were about to have dinner, there was a knock on the door. It was Mr Heelis with a casket containing the ashes. He just said, very quietly, 'You know what you have to do with these, Storey.'

Tom said, 'Yes, I know, I will do exactly what she told me.' They shook hands. Mr Heelis thanked him and turned away.

'I couldn't hold back the tears,' said Tom, and when he was telling me about it the tears welled up again in his blue eyes.

It was truly the end of an era.

Beatrix Potter's death was noted widely in the national press but my own favourite piece about her was written on Christmas Day 1943 by Delmar Banner, the local artist who, together with his wife, the sculptress Josephine De Vasconcellos, was a great friend of hers:

> All who knew Mrs Heelis will mourn a loved friend and a wise counsellor. All who knew her as 'Beatrix Potter' through her incomparable little books will mourn an artist of genius. I have met some who ask with astonishment, 'Did she do the pictures also?'. Who else could have done them? Their exquisite taste, free from all sentimentality, their sure observation, based on solid knowledge and their unique humour and charm, the flower of a rare and wonderful mind, will ensure them a perennial immortality. Many and many of us, who try in our own way to paint, acknowledge in Beatrix Potter a great artist, and it is our own clear waters, our own great fells, and the wild creatures of our fields and woods that live again in her lovely art. Her encouragement was given to us; our gratitude goes with her on her great journey.

One of the last fragments of Beatrix Potter's own handwriting, discovered in her house after her death, was the final verse of a poem about the Lakeland hills she loved so much:

> I will go back to the hills again
>   When the day's work is done,
> And set my hands against the rocks
>   Warm with an April sun,
> And see the night creep down the fells
>   And the stars climb one by one.

I had first come across this verse in 1942 when I produced a one-act play for the GFS called *Back to the Hills*. It was a very beautiful and sensitive play and in the last scene the main character had an emotive speech bringing in this particular verse. Imagine my surprise some thirty years later when I bought a copy of Leslie Linder's *A History of the Writings of Beatrix Potter* to find the whole poem there in his Introduction.

The next two years passed slowly for those of us waiting at home for our loved ones. From North Africa Jim had gone to Italy, and then to Greece. In May 1945, while he was still in Greece, VE [Victory in Europe] Day was declared and, although nothing in his letters suggested it, I naturally thought he would soon be coming home. Then, in August 1945, when VJ [Victory over Japan] Day was declared, I was certain he must be on his way back. However, it was not until September that the telephone rang. Jim was home. It seemed strange to hear his voice again.

'I'm catching the next train to Windermere,' he told me. 'I should arrive about noon, so please be there. I can't wait to see you.'

He had been demobbed at Ashton-under-Lyne and was taking the next train to Windermere. I must admit that I was a little apprehensive, but I

We celebrated VE Day with a trip round the villages on Bruce Dixon's wagon

was very excited at the same time. Jim Airey's taxi took me to meet the train and there was 'my' Jim, the same man I had married three years before. He had not changed at all.

Although Jim's civilian work was to be in the War Department at Western Command in Chester, he was given leave again until after Christmas, and we had three glorious months together in Near Sawrey before we had to settle down to what you might call a normal married life. After much searching round Chester, we found some furnished accommodation, which would see us through until we were able to move into an unfurnished flat. Although Chester is a beautiful city, steeped in history, I yearned to be back in Sawrey. Nowhere on earth could replace my country home.

It was while we were in Chester that we heard there was a stranger in Near Sawrey, knocking on everyone's door and asking a whole lot of questions about Mrs Heelis. The news travelled quickly that it was a woman called Margaret Lane, believed to be the Countess of Huntingdon and almost royalty! Everyone wanted to know the purpose of her questions.

'Don't encourage her, tell her nothing. She's making herself an awful nuisance at Castle Cottage. Poor Mr Heelis is fed-up with her continual presence there.'

We eventually learned, of course, that Margaret Lane was writing a biography of Beatrix Potter, and was seeking firsthand information. The villagers knew, however, that while she was still alive Mrs Heelis herself had been approached by Margaret Lane about the writing of her biography and her reply had been terse, to say the least.

'Mrs Heelis is a farmer, living in the North country of England, and has been happily married to William Heelis for thirty years. She breeds the little Herdwick sheep, suitable for grazing the fells of the Lake District. And that is all people need to know about me.'

Knowing that his wife had objected strongly to even the suggestion of a biography, Mr Heelis and the villagers were not at all prepared to cooperate with Margaret Lane. At last, in desperation, worn down by her continual persistence, Mr Heelis relented, and the villagers followed his lead in order that she would go away and leave them in peace. In 1946 *The Tale of Beatrix Potter* by Margaret Lane was published by Frederick Warne and for the first time the story of this remarkable woman was revealed.

William Heelis did not live to see the book's publication, nor its extraordinary success, for he had died in 1945, just eighteen months after his wife, in a nursing home in York. The new resident in Castle Cottage was one of Beatrix Potter's trustees, Captain Kenneth Duke, the husband of her cousin Stephanie Hyde Parker. Captain Duke had succeeded Bruce Thompson as the National Trust Area Agent and was working with Cubby Acland, then the chief agent for the National Trust in the Lake District.

That year the decision was taken by all the parties concerned that visitors to the Lake District might like to see where Beatrix Potter had written many of her children's books and to savour the atmosphere of the old seventeenth-century farmhouse which she had loved so much. So in July 1946 Hill Top was formally opened to the public, with Mrs Susan Ludbrook as its first Curator. All the local people were invited to a preview gathering at Hill Top, and many of their signatures can be found today in the old visitors' book. Fifty years later, those same people were invited by the then Administrator of Hill Top, Mike Hemming, to return for a grand celebration and reunion. Unfortunately I was absent for both occasions. In 1946 I was living in Chester, and in 1996 I was travelling in the United States of America. I was very sad that I missed two of the most important and enjoyable days in the history of the village.

A PROPERTY OF THE NATIONAL TRUST

HILL TOP, SAWREY

FORMERLY THE HOME OF BEATRIX POTTER

Open (during the Summer only)

WEEKDAYS: 10-30 a.m. to 6 p.m.   SUNDAYS: 2 p.m to 6 p.m.

ADMISSION 1/-   CHILDREN 6d.

MEMBERS OF THE NATIONAL TRUST FREE.

Entrance by the wicket gate close to the
Tower Bank Arms, Near Sawrey

Note.   The number of persons admitted to the house at any one time
will be strictly limited.

The first admission ticket to Hill Top, July 1946

That first year, 1946, Hill Top was open only in July, August and September, and during those three months 2,400 enthusiastic visitors were admitted. Opening the house had been looked upon purely as an experiment but the success of this trial run prompted the National Trust to open the property annually from Easter to September, seven days a week, and in 1970 this was increased to the end of October. Today, so great are the numbers of tourists wanting to visit Hill Top, that the opening times have had to be reduced again, to five days a week and six hours per day, in order to preserve the fabric of the tiny house.

Meanwhile, in Chester, Jim and I heard that a new Ministry had been formed, Pensions and National Insurance, and that there was to be an office in Windermere where they were looking for staff. Jim applied for a transfer from the War Department to the new Ministry and was accepted. Our eldest daughter, Helen, had been born in the Tower Bank Arms on 5 December 1947, so it was a happy day when, early the following year, we all moved back to Sawrey.

We lived in Rose Cottage, opposite St Peter's Church in Far Sawrey, in a house belonging to 'Gus' Tyson, who owned Town End Dairy Farm at Hawkshead. When we had approached him about it, he said, 'Of course you can lease it. Who better? You are the little girl who always used to wave to me on your journey to school in Hawkshead and you were always smiling!' They were happy days in Rose Cottage, and our son John was born on 23 September 1949 in Lanrigg Nursing Home in Bowness-on-Windermere, the last baby to be born there, for it closed down immediately afterwards.

Life, however, has its highs and its lows and in 1952, in what seemed to us like no time at all, Jim was transferred from Windermere to the Keswick office, some twenty miles from Sawrey. As we had no car, Jim had to cycle to Hawkshead, catch Jim Airey's bus to Ambleside and then take the Ribble bus to Keswick. He made the journey daily for a while, a long trek which made for a long day, but at last he managed to rent a new council house for us all in Keswick. Never, never do I want to live anywhere near a council estate again. The house itself was fine, with a big garden and fields at the back, but, oh dear, it was not for me. Whether it was fortunate or unfortunate that I became ill with thyroid trouble I cannot say, but the doctor advised me to leave Keswick if at all possible. It was not long before we were all back in Near Sawrey and Jim had returned to the Windermere office.

We moved into Meadowcroft, the original Ginger and Pickles shop, rented to us by the owner, Billy Kenyon. I served morning coffee and afternoon teas

Our children: (*right*) Helen, born December 1947; (*below left*) John, born September 1949; (*below right*) Jane, born April 1959

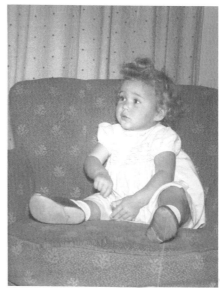

and applied to Frederick Warne for a licence to sell the Beatrix Potter books. Although the licence was granted, it came too late, for drastic changes were about to take place in our lives.

I was devastated when, in 1956, my mother died and my father moved out of the Tower Bank Arms into Croft End, a small cottage in Market Street, next door to my sister in Stoney Croft, the cottage that had been the old carpenter's shop. Sawrey would never be quite the same again. As the locals commented, 'Tower Bank Arms is finished. There's no sound of your mother's laughter, no welcome there any more.' Everybody had loved my mother. We had had three guest rooms at the Tower Bank Arms and could accommodate eight guests at any one time, sometimes even squeezing in one or two more if Betty and I went in with our mother and our father moved downstairs on to a camp bed. Although we only had one bathroom in the house, visitors would return to stay year after year and one entry in the visitors' book reads, 'It is not like home here. It is a thousand times better!'

So in 1956, after the big upheaval, we decided to leave the village and move to Leamington Spa, where we lived for the next sixteen years. Our youngest daughter, Jane, was born in Warnford Hospital on 11 April 1959. In 1958 we had acquired our beloved Corgi, Mandy, who lived happily with us until, at the ripe old age of eleven, Jim had the distressing job of taking her to the vet to be put to sleep. We all stayed at home weeping buckets of tears and on his return Jim said, 'No more dogs, please.' It wasn't until after Jim's death that I had another dog.

During those sixteen years in Leamington Spa I was so grateful for the excellent education which our three children received, for the little church of St Mary Magdalene at Lillington, and for the friendship of our neighbours. However, Sawrey was always uppermost in my mind.

3.

BACK TO THE HILLS AGAIN

There was another important event in Near Sawrey that I missed during the time we were in Leamington Spa. It was the occasion when, in 1970, the village was invaded by a large film crew. Led by the actor and director Bryan Forbes, E M I Studios were making a ballet film of Beatrix Potter's stories. Produced by Richard Goodwin and designed by Christine Edzard, the film featured the Royal Ballet, and the choreographer was the renowned Frederick Ashton, who also took the rôle of Mrs Tiggy-winkle.

When I saw *The Tale of the Tales* in Leamington the following year, I knew at once that Beatrix Potter would have approved. It was simply beautiful, the music, the periods of quiet, the scenery and, above all, the animal characters. They were charming, straight out of the books, just as if they had stepped off the pages, and when I saw Mrs Tiggy-winkle running across the field, happy memories came flooding back. The film made cinema history and has since been shown throughout the world. It is certainly a classic.

Frederick Ashton as Mrs Tiggy-winkle in *The Tale of the Tales*

After the release of the film, the number of visitors to Hill Top trebled, and the village was swamped with tourists. Even though the National Trust stated on its brochures 'NO COACHES', buses carrying forty to sixty passengers began to arrive and the only parking space for them was the small lay-by opposite the entrance to Hill Top which holds only about six cars. There was an urgent need to make a car park, but where? The site chosen was the old fruit orchard in Courier Yard, next to the timber yard. I was sad to know that the place where Margaret Dixon and I had scrumped apples was to be so changed, but it was well out of sight of the rest of the village and the cars and coaches would be camouflaged by the trees.

In November 1971, the year before Jim was due to retire from the Civil Service, we received the shocking news that Freda Jackson (*née* Storey), who had been the Curator of Hill Top since the retirement of Susan Ludbrook in 1958, had suddenly died. Freda had always been a great friend of mine. She had never moved away from Sawrey and, after the war, had married Ted Jackson, who had been brought up in The Eagle's Head, the village inn at Satterthwaite. Shattered by the news of Freda's death, we travelled back to Sawrey to attend her funeral in St Peter's Church on a most beautiful autumn day.

As was our normal practice whenever we visited Sawrey, we picked up a copy of the *Westmorland Gazette* to keep us up-to-date with the local news. In Leamington I settled down to read it and when I came to the 'Job Vacancies' I saw that the National Trust was advertising for a Warden for the Tarn Hows estate. I mentioned it casually to Jim, who seemed mildly interested, but as Tarn Hows is in a very remote spot and as local living accommodation went with the job, there was no further discussion on the subject just then. The following day, however, it was obvious that Jim had been giving it some thought.

'You know, that wouldn't be bad, that job with the National Trust,' he said. 'I am due to retire next year and it's possible that I could take early retirement.' Jim was a great joker and I felt sure he must be pulling my leg but he meant it, and we sent off for an application form.

The reply to our application came as a complete surprise. It stated that as Tarn Hows was such a vast area the job of Warden there required a much younger man, but if we would be interested in the Curatorship of Hill Top in Near Sawrey, would we attend the National Trust's Ambleside Office for an interview when convenient. We were interviewed by Christopher Hanson-Smith and Cubby Acland, and it was surely a Red Letter Day, for we were appointed. Jim was to continue his work in the Civil Service until

Hill Top as it was when first opened to the public

his due retirement date of June 1972; May Flack, who had worked at Hill Top for the past ten years, would act as Custodian until we arrived.

During this waiting period, Beatrix Potter's friend, Miss Hammond, sadly died. She had been living in The Castle, next door to Castle Cottage, and we were able to move in there. Our youngest daughter, Jane, who was attending Kenilworth Grammar School, was accepted at the Queen Elizabeth School in Kirby Lonsdale, although she would have to be a boarder. Our eldest daughter, Helen, had already married and emigrated to Western Australia, following our son John who had emigrated there in 1970.

Just to live in Sawrey again was a dream come true for me, but to pass by the Tower Bank Arms was a sad experience, for it was now run down and uncared for. The tenant at that time had become an alcoholic. He had an artificial leg, owing to a motorbike accident, and he seemed very bitter about his condition. I could not hold back the tears when I saw that my happy childhood home had been reduced to this.

There had been many other changes in the area since we had left in 1956. Sawrey School had closed in July 1969. The building had been renamed

Braithwaite Hall and was still being used for the main village activities, although the village institute opposite was in constant use for the men to play billiards and for the weekly whist-drives. The village children now attended Hawkshead School up to the age of eleven, and then moved on to either the John Ruskin School in Coniston or to the Lakes School in Windermere. Kelsick Grammar School in Ambleside had become part of the Charlotte Mason College for teacher training.

In 1971, during the last year of Freda Storey's Curatorship, Hill Top had been visited by nearly 50,000 people. In those days the entrance fees were taken and the little books were sold in the house, but it was becoming impossible to manage all that and, at the same time, to answer the many questions about Beatrix Potter. So the decision was made to build a shop (which the National Trust insisted must be called an entrance lodge, *not* a shop) at the bottom of the flag path, leading up to the house. By September the shop was completed and ready for trading. At first people in the village thought it was the public toilets, as there was no window facing the road. Mrs Bloomer, who lived in a bungalow directly opposite the building and was a staunch member of the National Trust, had eight blue hydrangeas planted to conceal the blank wall which had replaced the pretty fruit orchard.

Those first years as Curators at Hill Top were happy ones for both Jim and me. My husband was a very modest man, kind and tender-hearted. He thoroughly enjoyed working at Hill Top and meeting the visitors, especially

My husband, Jim, welcoming a Japanese visitor to Hill Top

64

We were always busy in the Hill Top shop

the children. As he was tall and had a grey bushy beard, they obviously thought he was the real Mr McGregor. I still receive letters from Japanese visitors addressed to 'Mrs McGregor'. Jim had that special quality of making people laugh no matter how miserable they were feeling, and he had the gift of tact in an awkward situation, something which was certainly needed when dealing with an irate customer. Jim was much respected by all who knew him.

Soon after we returned to Sawrey Jim had begun to suffer with angina, but it had not prevented him from leading an active and busy life. Suddenly, however, on 26 April 1980, when he was in his seventy-third year, Jim had a massive heart attack. He had been watching the football on television, something he did every Saturday evening, and as he got up quickly to go to the kitchen he just fell at my feet and died. It was a dreadful shock.

> After the dark there comes a dawning,
> And heavy snows will melt away,
> After the raindrops comes the sunlight,
> After night God sends the day.
>
> After heartbreak comes the stillness,
> After tears there comes a smile,
> After sorrow there is a healing
> And sweet peace comes after a while.

(Anon.)

Happily for Jim there was no suffering, which was a real blessing. I simply had to pick up the pieces and carry on. Continuing at Hill Top, I became the sole Administrator, the same job as Curator but with an increase of clerical work and with more responsibility. Being kept so busy was a great help; I had no time to grieve or to feel sorry for myself. It was not until I was alone in the evenings that I was able to give way to my feelings and let the tears flow. The neighbours were all very kind and I was thankful to be back in Sawrey, but if it had not been for my faith I would have crumbled. Sorrow is part of the cost of love and many precious memories of that love will remain with me for ever.

I replaced Jim as churchwarden in St Peter's Church and discovered what a big responsibility that position is, but I had Harry Byers to guide me and he was a very good teacher. In 1983 I was licensed by the Bishop to assist in the administration of the sacraments at Holy Communion.

My husband, Jim Taylor, in 1975

I stayed at Hill Top until 1985, and these were eventful years in the life of the village – and of the world of Beatrix Potter. In 1978 Dutton's Brewery had put the Tower Bank Arms on the market. Of the many offers to purchase the property that of the National Trust was the one accepted and work started immediately on renovation and restoration. The door to the right of the bay window was blocked up and the three rooms in the front of the house were made into one long room. These three rooms had been the sitting room (with the bay window) which is above the cellar, the public bar in the middle, and the little bar parlour at the end. The dining-room is now where our cobbled yard used to be.

A series of managers was then employed, until it was eventually decided to put in tenants. Philip and Dorothy Broadley have successfully restored the Tower Bank Arms to a pleasant, happy, and homely country inn. There are now three bedrooms, all with bathrooms en suite, and today's visitors to Hill Top and to the village enjoy calling in for bar meals and a good beer. There is always a very warm welcome.

In 1980 the Beatrix Potter Society was formed, founded by a number of people professionally involved in the curatorship of Beatrix Potter material, to promote the study and appreciation of her life. The Society grew quickly and now has nearly 1,000 Members in many parts of the world, including America, Canada, Australia, Holland, Italy, Russia and Japan. An International Study Conference is held every other year, usually at the Charlotte Mason College, Ambleside, now called St Martin's College and part of the University of Lancaster, and invariably some new information about Beatrix Potter, her life and work, is revealed by Conference speakers.

It was during 1980 that a certain American lady visited Hill Top for the first time. She had become interested in the life of Beatrix Potter after reading Margaret Lane's biography, and she had read all the stories as a child. Jacqueline Mock had already visited Warne, the publishers, in London seeking further information and she was advised by them to travel to Near Sawrey and to ask for Willow Taylor at Hill Top. At once I detected in her a genuine fascination for Peter Rabbit and his creator. She asked me numerous questions, and then simply did not want to leave. It was the beginning of a wonderful friendship and, for me, a new era was on the horizon.

On her return home Jacqueline was invited to present a programme on Beatrix Potter at her local library in New Jersey. After some hesitation she agreed and it was a great success. The news of her presentation, 'The Amazing Beatrix Potter', spread to schools and libraries in other parts of

One of Jacqueline Mock's flyers

America and Jacqueline soon found she was being asked to repeat her programme across the United States. One year she invited me to come and read the Beatrix Potter Tales to the younger children in the schools and libraries, while she presented her programme to the higher grades. Consequently I began my regular visits to her home in New Jersey, and to Pennsylvania, where she has a lovely old farmhouse.

Meanwhile, our daughter Jane, who had been working as a nanny near the house of an old schoolfriend, Diane Elwood, had become friendly with her brother, Robert. In no time at all they had become engaged, and in 1982 they married. He is a farmer from Warcop, near Appleby, and their farm, Rowend, is just about half-a-mile from Judith and Michael Heelis. As Michael is the great, great nephew of William Heelis, our family is still in close contact with the Heelis family.

Also in 1982 a film crew from the BBC arrived in Near Sawrey to make a documentary of Beatrix Potter's life based on Margaret Lane's book. The film was narrated by Michael Hordern and Penelope Wilton played Beatrix Potter. The villagers, including me, were invited to appear in some of the scenes and it was great fun being part of it all. When the making of the film

I was one of the extras in the BBC's 1982 documentary *The Tale of Beatrix Potter*

was over, we had a very jolly farewell party in the Rothay Manor in Ambleside, dancing the night away with some of the folk-dances which Mr Heelis had enjoyed so many years before.

Every new retelling of the story of Beatrix Potter's life and every extra piece of publicity results in an increase in the number of visitors to Hill Top. We were opening six-and-a-half days a week, Monday to Saturday and on Sunday afternoons, and in 1984 we reached the record number of 90,000 visitors in the seven months from Easter to the end of October. The continuing pressure on the property and on the village was becoming so great that something had to be done to ease the situation. The number of days and the hours of opening were gradually decreased and alterations were made to the lay-out of the property and garden. There was also serious concern about the condition and safety of the Beatrix Potter original watercolours on display in the New Room at Hill Top and in 1983 they were removed for conservation and safekeeping. The result was a public outcry and a series of bitter complaints, particularly by those who had travelled halfway round the world to see them, and we found ourselves with a great deal of explaining to do.

I remained as Administrator of Hill Top until the National Trust replaced me in 1985, and I was then employed on a seasonal, part-time basis three days a week at Hill Top and three days at the National Trust Information Centre in Hawkshead, but it was not until 1987 that the National Trust found the solution to the problem of how to display its Beatrix Potter originals.

Next door to the Red Lion Hotel, in the centre of the quaint old village of Hawkshead, was where William Heelis, Solicitors, had had their offices since the end of the 19th century. It was also the place where Beatrix Potter had met her future husband for the first time. On his death William Heelis had left the building to the National Trust, on condition that it remained a solicitors' office for as long as required, and until 1987 it had been tenanted by Gatey Heelis, Solicitors. When this firm decided to leave, the National Trust seized the opportunity. This would be the ideal place to exhibit Beatrix Potter's original work. Although the building had been preserved much as it was at the turn of the century, complete with its original furniture, a programme of careful work began and it was another year before the house was ready to open to the public. The creation of the Gallery was made possible by a generous donation from Frederick Warne and with the aid of grants from The English Tourist Board, The Council for Rural Development and North West Museums and Art Gallery Service.

Next door to the Gallery is a very small, square building, drawn by Beatrix Potter in *The Tale of the Pie and the Patty-Pan* as Tabitha Twitchit's little shop. For many years this had been the National Trust Information Centre and it was now to be the ticket office for the Gallery and a recruitment centre for the National Trust. I became the full-time ticket seller and recruiter.

Mrs W Taylor

THE NATIONAL TRUST
and
FREDERICK WARNE

REQUEST THE PLEASURE OF YOUR COMPANY
AT THE OFFICIAL OPENING OF

THE BEATRIX POTTER GALLERY, HAWKSHEAD

AT 12 NOON
ON THURSDAY 28 JULY
THE ANNIVERSARY OF BEATRIX POTTER'S BIRTHDAY

Please meet in the
Town Hall, The Square,
Hawkshead

Buffet Lunch

PLEASE REPLY TO:
THE NATIONAL TRUST
ROTHAY HOLME
ROTHAY ROAD
AMBLESIDE, CUMBRIA
BY FRIDAY 8 JULY

FROM THE PIE AND THE PATTY PAN
BY BEATRIX POTTER
© FREDERICK WARNE 1905

My invitation to the opening of the Beatrix Potter Gallery in Hawkshead

On 28 July 1988, as a fitting celebration of the anniversary of Beatrix Potter's birth on 28 July 1866, the National Trust held the opening ceremony for the Beatrix Potter Gallery. In spite of the heavy rain, it was a most memorable occasion. A rope woven from Herdwick wool, looped across the doorway, was cut by Geoff Storey, Tom Storey's son, with sheep shears which were in use on Hill Top Farm when Mrs Heelis was alive and which are still in use today. Among the 120 guests present were many of the tenant farmers from the farms that had been owned by Beatrix Potter and which she had left to the National Trust on her death.

Geoff Storey opening the Gallery

Tom Storey, Beatrix Potter's shepherd, had died just before Easter 1986 at the age of ninety. A popular man in the village and with the local farmers, his expertise and knowledge about the breeding of Herdwick sheep had been sought throughout the area. After he retired from Hill Top, Tom had continued to value flocks of Herdwicks for the National Trust when its farms changed tenants, as Beatrix Potter had willed that a certain number of sheep had always to be handed on to the incoming tenant. Tom had been laid to rest in the picturesque churchyard of Jesus Church at Troutbeck, beside his wife Hilda and his daughter Freda.

Only three months after the opening of the Beatrix Potter Gallery, the village was stunned to hear of the sudden death of Geoff Storey at the age of sixty-five. Geoff and I were exactly the same age and we had attended the village school together. He had lived at Hill Top Farm for sixty-two years and held the tenancy for forty-two of them. On leaving school, and even before that, he had worked alongside his father under the watchful eye of Beatrix Potter, who was always very fond of Geoff and could see the potential for a very good shepherd in him. Under the caring supervision of Tom, Geoff had indeed become a sheep specialist and an authority on the Herdwick, and he died doing what he did best, looking after his flock.

On the day of his funeral, 17 October 1988, the little church of St Peter's, Far Sawrey, was packed with all his friends, relatives and members of the farming fraternity from throughout the district. We listened as Gordon Hall, then Regional Land Agent for the National Trust, read Gray's 'Elegy written in a Country Churchyard':

> The curfew tolls the knell of parting day,
> The lowing herd wind slowly o'er the lea,
> The plowman homeward plods his weary way,
> And leaves the world to darkness, and to me.

> *   *   *

> Large was his bounty, and his soul sincere,
> Heav'n did a recompense as largely send:
> He gave to Mis'ry all he had, a tear:
> He gain'd from Heav'n ('twas all he wish'd) a friend.

In his address, Canon Southward said, 'Talking to the local people about Geoff Storey two words have surfaced, *patience* and *tenderness*,' and then he quoted from *The Good Life* by John Manningham: 'Wilt thou be a King? Be a shepherd, thou hast subjects, thou hast sheep, thou hast a sceptre, thou hast a crook ... Thy companions are the sun, the moon, and the stars ... He that was God's second best beloved was a shepherd and a King; if thou art a shepherd, thou art a King ... '

On a serene autumn afternoon, when the surrounding countryside was adorned with shades of gold, bronze, yellow, red and green, Geoff Storey was laid to rest in Sawrey churchyard. A flock of sheep in the neighbouring field lay quietly on the hillside looking up to Heaven; it was as if they too mourned his passing.

In July 1991 a most important visitor arrived in Sawrey. Henry P. Coolidge had travelled from Boston, U.S.A., on a nostalgic visit to Hill Top and Castle Cottage, where he had first met Beatrix Potter sixty-four years earlier, when he was a thirteen-year-old boy. Henry P. and his mother, given an

The guinea-pig, Tuppeny, having his hair combed by Xarifa in *The Fairy Caravan*

introduction to Beatrix Potter by a New England artist friend, had been invited to take tea at Castle Cottage. Henry P. was familiar with all the Tales; in fact, he knew most of them by heart. He also loved animals almost as much as Beatrix Potter did, so it was hardly surprising that they became friends.

During that afternoon in 1927 Beatrix Potter had taken Henry P. and his mother over to Hill Top to show them the places illustrated in her books. She had brought out her portfolios of drawings, given him some of her watercolours and then asked him which pictures he thought she might use in a new book. He had suggested a story about guinea-pigs, because he kept guinea-pigs and those were the pictures he liked best. His suggestion came to fruition in *The Fairy Caravan*, which was first published in America in 1929, although not published in England until 1952, nine years after the author's death. The book is dedicated to Henry P. and its preface reads, 'Through many changing seasons these tales have walked and talked with me. They were not meant for printing; I have left them in the homely idiom of our north country speech. I send them on the insistence of friends beyond the sea. Beatrix Potter.'

That first meeting with Beatrix Potter in 1927 had resulted in a life-long friendship with the Coolidge family and with other visitors from New England. The sales in America of a series of specially painted animal pictures enabled Beatrix Potter to contribute funds to the National Trust to buy Cockshott Point, glebe land on the shores of Windermere, to save it from building developers.

An early photograph of Sawrey residents skating on Esthwaite Water:
(*from left*) George Devon, Mary Postlethwaite, Mollie Green, Jack Byers
and Harry Byers, *c.*1930

On his 1991 visit, Henry Coolidge came on from Hill Top to the Beatrix
Potter Gallery in Hawkshead and there he was amazed to discover that I
was one of the last remaining residents – along with Mollie Green, Alan
Brockbank and Harry Byers – who had been living in Sawrey at the time of
his first visit in 1927. We reminisced for long together about the time when
Beatrix Potter was alive and Henry P. recalled many happy memories of
the Lake District so many years before.

In November 1991 the village was saddened by the death of Harry Byers,
Mollie Green's eldest brother, who was one of the most popular and
respected inhabitants of Sawrey, where he had lived for the whole of his
ninety-one years. When he was fourteen, Harry started working for Beatrix
Potter in the garden at Hill Top Farm, and he stayed there for thirteen
years before leaving to take up full-time gardening. When he retired at the
age of sixty-five, Harry returned to Hill Top, this time as the gardener
employed by the National Trust.

Visitors loved to talk to him about Beatrix Potter and one of the stories he
used to tell was about old Mrs Potter coming by carriage from her house on
the other side of Windermere to visit her daughter at Castle Cottage every
Wednesday afternoon.

'I never saw that old woman smile,' he recalled. 'She always looked miserable and she never stayed long. You could set your watch by her arrival and departure.'

I am glad to know that all Harry's stories have been recorded and safely stored away in the National Trust sound archives. He was one of our local characters who will always live in our memories. He was a modest gentleman but one of the true greats, greater than he knew. He was laid to rest in Sawrey churchyard, opposite the door of St Peter's, where he was churchwarden for forty years.

In the middle of the tourist season in 1992 a man called in to the Beatrix Potter Gallery asking for me. He was from Border Television and had been advised by one of the local Sawrey residents that I would be the most suitable person to tell him about Beatrix Potter. His name was Harry King and he was the producer and director of *Highway*, a television programme of hymns and interviews from different regions of the United Kingdom shown weekly on ITV. Would I appear on the programme and be interviewed by Sir Harry Secombe? How could I refuse?

I was interviewed by Sir Harry Secombe for *Highway* in the Entrance Hall at Hill Top in 1992

So in November of that year the interview was filmed in the Entrance Hall at Hill Top. I was very nervous appearing with such a famous star as Sir Harry, but I need not have been. He has the wonderful gift of making you feel at ease and relaxed in his presence and he also has a great sense of humour.

The programme was full of song and spectacular scenery. The sun enhanced the superb beauty of the autumn colours. It was perfect. Among the other people interviewed were Bill Rollinson, the Lakeland historian, Bruce Hanson, the curator of Brantwood, the home of Ruskin, and Chris Bonnington, the famous Cumbrian mountaineer and a great supporter of the National Trust. For me, the outstanding item on the programme was Faith Elliot, who stood on a jetty on Coniston Water singing Dvořák's 'Song to the Moon' from *Rusalka*. Faith is the daughter of Canon Colin Elliot, one time vicar of St Martin's, Bowness-on-Windermere, and she has been singing from childhood. The next item after my interview at Hill Top was the actress Jean Anderson reading Beatrix Potter's famous story letter to Noel Moore about Peter Rabbit, and it was obvious that she had told this story to children many times before. That edition of *Highway* was voted the best of the series in 1992 and won an award for Border Television. I was very proud to be part of it.

4.

THE FINAL MILESTONE

I retired on 29 October 1993, five months after my seventieth birthday, and my job was taken over by members of the Gallery staff, who worked alternately in the Gallery or the Ticket Office. At a little ceremony at the Gallery I was presented with my own choice of book, '*So I shall tell You a Story...*', edited by Judy Taylor. I love reading about all the various encounters with Beatrix Potter.

In 1985 I had moved out of The Castle and into Stoney Lane Cottage next door, which was also owned by the National Trust. As the new cottage was only half the size of the old one, a lot of items, such as books and china, had been stored in boxes in the garage and several months went by after my retirement before I began to sort everything out. It was then that I discovered the garage roof had been leaking and many of the books were ruined. However, at the bottom of one box and protected by other volumes, were two grey, paperback books of folk-dances, with instructions and diagrams on how to do them. Both were inscribed 'Heelis, Castle Cottage, Sawrey'. They had been given to me years ago and long forgotten.

I posted them off straight away to Judy Taylor, then the Chairman of the Beatrix Potter Society, because I knew the Society would treasure and preserve them. It was not long before one of the Society's International Study Conferences was due in Ambleside and the discovery of the books led to a memorable, and somewhat hilarious, evening of folk-dancing at the Conference – the first time for the majority of the delegates. I am glad to say that the books are now part of the extensive Beatrix Potter Collection at the Victoria and Albert Museum in London. I feel so strongly that we must try to keep these really English items here in England, especially those associated with Beatrix Potter.

In 1993 there were celebrations in many parts of the world to mark the centenary of the Peter Rabbit picture letter, which had been written on 4 September 1893. I was staying with Jacqueline Mock in the spring of that year, when she was invited by Royal Doulton to do an extensive tour for them in the various big cities of the United States. They were sending over two artists from England to demonstrate the painting of the Beatrix Potter figurines and they wanted Jacqueline to accompany them into the big department stores. However, as she was already so heavily booked with programmes and it would be impossible for her to undertake any more appointments, she suggested that I might go instead to talk about Beatrix Potter and to read the stories. When Royal Doulton heard that there was

Amanda Clifford's design for the Peter Rabbit Centenary logo

an English woman right there on the spot who had actually known Beatrix Potter, they agreed without hesitation.

The tour started on 24 March. We travelled to Dallas, Texas, then to Houston, and on to Washington, D.C. The next stop was Philadelphia and then on to New York City to read the stories in F.A.O. Schwarz, the famous toyshop. Here I had a variety of audiences, including a group of teenage students who were thoroughly enjoying themselves. Sitting round me on the floor they asked for a story, so I read them *The Tale of Jemima Puddle-Duck*. When I came to the part where the sandy whiskered gentleman shows Jemima into the shed full of feathers, one young man put up his hand.

'Does this story have a happy ending? It sounds a bit suspect to me.'

I assured him that he need have no worries and continued. As soon as they knew that Kep and the hounds had saved Jemima, they all clapped and cheered. What a fine group of youngsters they were.

Finally, the tour took me to Cincinnati and to Louisville and in each store someone was dressed as a Beatrix Potter character, Peter Rabbit, Jemima Puddle-duck or Tom Kitten. The children were fascinated by my accent, one little boy saying, 'You talk different. Where do you come from?' It was all great fun, and I loved every minute.

Back in Sawrey, I kept myself occupied working in the garden and walking Susie, the much-loved little dog I had had since 1988. That year I had been staying with my daughter, Jane, in Warcop and we had seen an advertisement in the window of a pet shop in Appleby: 'Good home wanted for a young Jack Russell Terrier'. Encouraged by Jane, who knew that I had longed to have another dog ever since my little Corgi, Mandy, had died in 1969, I telephoned the number in the advertisement. When three-year-old Susie was brought along to Jane's house, we all fell in love with her, especially Jane's children, and I took her with me when I returned home.

Now, however, I soon realised that gardening and walking Susie were not enough to keep me occupied and that I hated the thought of losing contact with people, with the National Trust and with the tale of Beatrix Potter. So I became a National Trust volunteer, working every Sunday afternoon recruiting members and issuing tickets at Townend, Troutbeck, the latter a particular pleasure because of Townend being my ancestral home.

A painting of Townend by Pat Bell

I also started going to the Beatrix Potter Gallery in Hawkshead once a week during the school holidays to read the Beatrix Potter Tales to children. One day a little girl came in dressed exactly as Beatrix Potter had dressed as a child. I could not believe what I was seeing. I was amazed. She asked me if I would like to hear her tell the story of Peter Rabbit.

'I would love that,' I said, 'and I'm sure all the other people would like to hear it, too.'

She told it beautifully, without looking at the book. What could be more rewarding than sharing the wonderful, enchanting world of childhood?

Another of my retirement occupations was to guide groups of tourists round the places in Near Sawrey associated with Beatrix Potter, especially those that appear in the illustrations to her books. They were fascinated to see how little those places had changed over the years. They were also delighted to have a guide who actually knew Beatrix Potter and could give them a personal account of her. But one day, quite suddenly and without warning, my bones began to creak and my knees became very painful. It was the onset of arthritis. Then my breath became short. It was angina. I realised that it would be folly to stay in a cottage with so many steps and stairs and that, when the day came that I could not drive, I would be stranded, for there was no longer any public transport to or from Near Sawrey. I would have to find a ground-floor flat somewhere.

Recently I had been visiting an old Sawrey friend, Helen Atkinson, in her beautiful retirement flat in Calgarth Park, Troutbeck Bridge, a handsome building on the far shore of Windermere, which had originally been the home of Richard Watson, Bishop of Llandaff, 'the absent Bishop'. At the beginning of this century the Calgarth Estate was bought by Oswald Hedley who, during the First World War, gave the house to be used as a convalescent home, firstly for Belgian wounded and then for British officers and, when his widow died in 1916, it was named The Ethel Hedley Hospital in her memory. In 1920 it became The Ethel Hedley Orthopaedic Hospital, with twenty beds for disabled children, and in 1924 it was considerably extended so that it could accommodate fifty children. By 1970, due to the setting-up of the National Health Service, there was no further use for the hospital and it was closed.

It remained empty until the Lake District Branch of the British Federation of University Women formed the Lake District Housing Association and converted the house into twenty-six flats for retired professional people, with a warden and a communal dining-room. Calgarth Park was officially opened with a garden party on 19 June 1974.

Part of Calgarth Park into which I moved in 1996

On one of my visits to Helen Atkinson I had remarked on the beauty of the place and said how much I would like to live there one day. She told me that there was a long waiting list and that I should put my name down as soon as possible. Sadly, Helen died in 1995 so I was not able to be in residence while she was there, but I moved in to her lovely flat on 1 April 1996 and, with my superb view across the lake to Claife Heights and beyond, I feel that I am not too far from home. Susie came with me when I first moved in but now, at the considerable age of fourteen, she is living with my daughter on the farm.

I am still fully occupied with voluntary work for the National Trust at Townend and at the Hawkshead Gallery and since 1997 I have added the Armitt Library in Ambleside to my list, working one half-day a week in the new Museum. The Armitt Library was founded in 1912 'to create a collection of books of scientific, literary or antiquarian value for the student and book-lover' and Beatrix Potter had been a subscribing member since its start. In 1933, shortly after her mother's death, she gave many of the books from her father's library to the Armitt, and in 1935 she presented a portfolio of her paintings, which contained remarkable watercolour studies of Roman artefacts she had made in London in 1894. After her death in 1943, hundreds of her exquisite fungus watercolours were given to the Armitt Library in compliance with her expressed wish, and they are now

Princess Alexandra with Eileen Jay at the opening of the new
Armitt Library and Museum in 1998

housed in the handsome new Armitt Library and Museum at Low Nook,
which was opened by Princess Alexandra in 1998. Although there are
many other fine books and paintings to be found there, it is the Beatrix
Potter connection that gives me the greatest joy.

My volunteer work brings me into contact with so many different people
and answers my need not to expend too much physical energy but to keep
my mind active. I now have one artificial hip and the other one is due for
replacement. As for my knees, they must wait. As David Kossoff writes in
'Young Mind' from '*You have a minute, Lord?*', a collection of poems which
he calls 'A sort of prayer book':

> What if the *mind* gets stiff in the joints?
>   Where are you then?
>
> *   *   *
>
> If creaky I must be, and many-spectacled,
>   and morning-stiff and food-careful,
>
> *   *   *
>
> I won't complain. Not a word.
> If, with your help, dear Friend, there
>   will dwell in this ancient monument,
> A Young Mind. Please, Lord?

I still have my little car which frequently takes me across the lake to Sawrey and whenever I am there my mind goes back to times past. How things have changed! In 1988 the two Sawreys were designated a Conservation Area, with many of the buildings being listed Grade II, which means they are of special interest and warrant every effort being made to preserve them. Hill Top, the Tower Bank Arms and Castle Cottage are all listed buildings.

There were five farms in the area of Near Sawrey at one time, but now Hill Top and Belle Green are the only two surviving working farms. High Green Gate is a guest-house, Dub Howe has been converted into three cottages, and Esthwaite Howe is a complex of holiday cottages and bungalows. In Far Sawrey there are just two farms left, Fold Farm and Hawkrigg Farm at the top of Ferry Hill. It was the farms that employed many of the men who lived in the cottages which are now holiday homes and only occupied for a few weeks of the year; hence the whole character of the village has changed beyond recognition. Young men and women who marry are forced to leave the villages to find work and living accommodation elsewhere.

The loss of the village school and the village church were two other drastic changes in the Sawreys. Another great change, common to many other parts of the country, is the lack of public transport in the area. When tourists arrive at Windermere Station and ask for directions to Beatrix Potter's house, they are told that it is in the village of Near Sawrey, 'just on the other side of the lake'. So they cross over on the ferry and believe they have arrived in Near Sawrey, not realising that there are a further two miles to go, with a long walk up the steep Ferry Hill.

There has been a ferry operating across Windermere for several hundred years. In the early days the ferries were rowed barges, used frequently by the monks of Furness Abbey. Then came the Windermere horse-ferry, an important connecting link for traffic from the Sawrey and Coniston side of Windermere to Kendal. In 1870 the first steam ferry came into service, pulling itself across by chain, and later by steel cable.

In 1912 Beatrix Potter wrote a letter to *Country Life* to complain that the testing of hydroplanes on the lake was a danger to the ferry service:

> ... Heavy laden with the Coniston four-horsed coach and char-à-banc, or with carrier's tilt cart and bustling motor, or homely toppling loads of oak bark and hooper's swills, or droves of sheep and cattle. Farm-carts go down and across with sacks of wool and bark and faggots; they struggle homewards with loads of coal. Everyone uses the ferry.

Horses crossing Windermere on the ferry on their way to the Hawkshead Show, *c*.1936

In 1915 there was a new steam ferry, larger and more up-to-date, with cabin accommodation and room for four motor cars. This lasted until 1954, when yet another new ferry, 'Drake', was launched, capable of carrying up to ten cars. The present ferry is 'Mallard', launched in 1990 with a capacity for eighteen cars and a hundred passengers, but still the queues grow and the wait for the ferry can be as long as an hour on either side of the lake.

Johnny Atkinson was the first ferryman I can remember. Always popular with both the locals and the tourists, he retired in 1938 at the age of seventy-two after twenty-eight years of service. His successor was Joss Hartley, who piloted the boat until his death in 1957, and he was followed by Jack Bowman who retired in the late 1970s. Since then there has been a succession of ferrymen, but none of them have reigned as long as the old ones.

Near Sawrey would hardly be known if it were not for the success of Beatrix Potter's illustrated Tales. The quiet corners of the village, its lanes, cottages, gates and doorways are now well recognised and familiar to visitors from all over the world. Tourism has completely taken over in this area, as it has in most areas of the Lake District. The true natives of the idyllic village of Near Sawrey find it hard to be tolerant, especially with the quantity of traffic and the number of people who descend upon them in July and

August each year. On the other hand the tourist industry is many people's bread and butter. Once upon a time 'Sheep were our bread', but not any more.

However, we cannot deny those poor folks who live in the inner cities the opportunity for a taste of life in the beautiful Lake Country. It always makes me think of *The Tale of Johnny Town-Mouse*. 'One place suits one person, another place suits another person. For my part I prefer to live in the country, like Timmy Willie.' (*See below.*) When I am reading this particular story to children, I usually add, 'Don't you?' and there is a loud chorus of 'YES!', followed by a discussion of where each person lives.

For me the loss of the vicarage of St Peter's Church in Far Sawrey was the greatest sadness. The Church has always been an integral part of my life and I loved the little church on the hill. Sunday School for the children was held at the back of the church every Sunday morning and I enjoyed it, but we always had to stay on for the morning service and I simply hated those long sermons. They were for the adults and I couldn't understand them. Worst of all I was expected to sit quietly, not moving an eye-lid, which was purgatory. We had the same two teachers for Sunday School as for day school and we were given

Canon Murray blessing the Hill Top cattle at Rogationtide

a stamp to stick into our attendance book, which of course encouraged us to attend, as we did not like empty spaces in our books.

I was confirmed in St Michael and All Angels in Hawkshead at the age of fourteen, all the girls wearing white dresses and head-dresses like nurses, but after confirmation I gradually fell away from attending church, only going on special festivals and saints' days. Pressures of school sports matches and other interests, and haytime and harvest work, meant Sundays were spent doing my homework. But my interest in the church and my faith remained.

I have seen five vicars come and go in Far Sawrey, the Rev. Spencer being the first one. He married us in 1942 and also christened our eldest daughter, Helen, in 1947. Canon Murray succeeded him and he christened our son, John, in 1949 and our youngest daughter, Jane, in 1961. When we arrived back to live in Near Sawrey in 1972, Canon David Ellis was the priest in charge and he stayed until 1975, being the last vicar to occupy the vicarage at St Peter's. There was a long interregnum before the Rev. Moorhouse joined us in 1976, during which time the vicarage had been sold. The whole village was united against the decision by the diocese to sell the large house, mainly because we feared it would become another holiday complex. It did. We also feared that this might be the end of church life altogether in the two Sawreys, so I wrote 'A Lament on the Loss of Sawrey Vicarage' and sent it to the bishop, at that time Bishop Halsey:

Oh, Sawrey! dearest of all villages,
Nestling 'midst Lakeland hills,
You are a refuge for city dwellers,
You are a jewel of great worth.
God has endowed us with this precious gift that we may nurture all who
    dwell within its boundaries, and they in turn may carry forth a deeper
    faith, a deeper love, and a much greater concern.
For it is within the village that the deepest roots can grow,
The village school, the village church,
These are the solid foundations on which Christian lives are built.
Can anyone from without say what's good for those who dwell within?
Can they really know the feeling,
The sincerity with which we pray
That every place in all the world
May be a Heaven on earth some day?

To keep our identity is no selfish desire,
But a hope for the rest of the world.
A hope that some light may shine forth from this village,
Spreading its rays like those of the sun,
Over the whole of the earth.
We've lost our school, our vicarage is threatened.
Please! may we keep our Parish and may we keep our church,
Where we as one body may worship the Lord,
And grow in Grace, in Love, in Faith,
And spread his name abroad.
The village is the country's heart,
Which keeps beating through each crisis.
If the heart is strong we're bound to win.
Don't weaken those roots from which Christianity grows.

This is false economy
Please! Think again!

St Peter's Church, Far Sawrey, where I was married and our children were christened

My plea did not even merit a reply. However, the Rev. Moorhouse came, with his wife, to live in Glebe House, next door to the Hawkshead vicarage. So we were fortunate to retain our own vicar in Far Sawrey, even though he was living two miles away. He stayed with us for five years but that was the end of Sawrey as a separate ministry, for we became part of a shared ministry with Hawkshead, Wray and Graythwaite, in the care of Canon Ambrose Southward. The present vicar is Canon Stephen Pye, who joined us in 1998. I love our church and my poem 'St Peter's Church, Far Sawrey' expresses the part it has played in my life.

As a child I walked along the path by the river to church.
I dawdled, picked flowers, and listened to the music of the water rippling
   over the stones,
I had the time to stand and stare and to listen.
Unaware of God's presence then.

Now, caught up in the rush of adult life,
I have to race to church in a car,
Seeing only other vehicles racing along the road.
But, with a deep awareness, that when I arrive and kneel in prayer
The still waters of God are within my heart.

Susie and me in the porch of Anvil Cottage with Mollie Green in 1992

St Peter's churchyard is the resting place for many of my friends. Mollie Green died peacefully on 2 February 1999 and was laid to rest there three days later on a bitterly cold day. True to Lakeland tradition, all her friends and relations gathered afterwards in the Sawrey Hotel for some warming refreshments and to reminisce on her long, useful and interesting life.

Mollie had been a member of the church choir from an early age until it was disbanded in the 1980s, and she was always singing as she went about her work. She loved St Peter's Church and was so disappointed when the congregations fell to about half-a-dozen. She was still bicycling when she was eighty, and would have continued to do so had it not been for the volume of traffic on the roads. Her husband, Edmund, had died on his tricycle in 1979, competing in a race in Lancashire at the age of seventy-two. Mollie was devastated but continued serving the visitors who came back year after year for her wonderful hospitality. Six years ago, when she was ninety, Mollie had a bad fall and broke her femur. From then her health began to deteriorate, but even though she was walking with a zimmer-frame, she continued to entertain her regular visitors. She would say, 'You put the kettle on and make some tea, and I'll get the biscuits and the cakes.' There was always a warm welcome at Anvil Cottage.

On sunny days in summer Mollie sat in her porch and visitors came from near and far to stop by and have a chat. She could tell them so much about Beatrix Potter. Her favourite story was about the time she went to see Mrs Heelis during the Second World War to ask if she could work on the farm. If she didn't get work she would have to take in evacuees – and this she was not happy about. Mrs Heelis said, 'Goodness! You aren't strong enough to do farm work, but I can get you another job.' She immediately picked up the telephone and rang Brathay Hall in Ambleside, into which a school from the south had been evacuated.

'Do you want a good cook? I've got the very person here with me now.'

Mollie was speechless, for she had not even been consulted on the matter. However, she ended up cycling from Near Sawrey to Ambleside and back, fourteen miles a day, four days a week, winter and summer, for the remainder of the war.

Mollie was a true Sawrey character and it was a sad day for everyone when she had to go to a nursing home in Keswick, leaving Anvil Cottage which had been her home for most of her ninety-six years. Although she lives on in our memories, that corner of Near Sawrey will never be quite the same again.

Through knowing Beatrix Potter my circle of friends has greatly widened and has spread to far distant lands. I have travelled down many avenues and experienced adventures of which I could never have dreamed. I sometimes wonder how Beatrix Potter would react if she were to return to Sawrey and see Hill Top as it is today. Hill Top was her shrine, full of her special treasures. She had left several notes about the place with instructions as to what must be done after her death and where certain items were to remain. It is my belief that she would not be too pleased with the scene today. She never liked crowds of people; she liked the peace and

Beatrix Potter with Tom Storey, examining her sheep in Post Office Meadow
– one of the last photographs taken of her

tranquillity of the village. She would probably oust everybody and she would
certainly turn the tables in the shop – the Entrance Lodge! She used to sit for
hours on Castle Rock, the promontory above Hill Top, sketching and
meditating. From there she could view the whole village and the full length
of Esthwaite Water. Another favourite place where she could be alone was
in the little Jesus Church in Troutbeck, where she could sit quietly and
hear only the bleating of the sheep.

When I visited Near Sawrey recently the Post Office Meadow was full of
sheep with their new lambs and my mind wandered back to my childhood.
In my imagination I saw Beatrix Potter with her shepherd's crook and her
clogs, the familiar sack around her shoulders. She stopped to examine and
admire her flock and then she went through Tom Kitten's gate, up the flag
path to Hill Top. I was too arthritic to climb the wall.

Epilogue

When you open the box of memories
You find treasures of silver and gold,
Riches which money can never buy,
Good friends, happy times, and dreams you've seen come true.
As the journey through life becomes shorter,
And we reach the Autumn of our years,
We are able to recollect and rediscover
God's Blessings among our Souvenirs.

(Willow Taylor)

The moving finger writes; and having writ
Moves on; nor all thy Piety nor Wit
Shall lure it back to cancel half a line,
Nor all thy Tears wash out a Word of it.

(Omar Khayyam)

INDEX

Page numbers in italics refer to illustrations